DARK STORM, GOLDEN JOURNEY

Dark Storm, *Golden Journey*

A Remarkable Spiritual Search for Inner Peace

Alison Demarco

MAINSTREAM
PUBLISHING

EDINBURGH AND LONDON

First published in Great Britain in 1999 by
MAINSTREAM PUBLISHING COMPANY (EDINBURGH) LTD
7 Albany Street
Edinburgh EH1 3UG

ISBN 1 84018 151 6

A catalogue record for this book is available from the British Library

Typeset in Sabon and Garamond
Printed and bound in Finland by WSOY

Acknowledgements

I would like to thank Midi Fairgrieve for her dedication in helping me to write this book, and for being part of my transformational journey. I would also like to thank Cathy Wilson for her wise guidance. Many thanks must also go to: Daryl, Tara, Ramon, Mum, Bill (Dad), Moyra (Moira), Tracy, Vic Spence, Jane Nottage, Brigid Gallagher, Dr Muriel Mackay (deceased), Vicky Wall (deceased), Harry Oldfield, Colin Read, Dionne Quinn, Denise Lilley, Fiona Gardiner, Kay Devine, Maureen O'Hare, Mohsinah Underwood, Marilyn Graham, Robert Fife, David Fraser, Brian Wallace, the man of "Understanding" – Andrew (Ilbert) Collingwood – and to all my friends and associates. Special thanks to the World of Colour, Natural and Spiritual Healing.

For those who want to know more about the Natural Healing and Spiritual Development Centre in Scotland's historic Roslin Glen, please contact:

Firth Lodge
Firth Road
Auchendinny
EH26 0QZ

Telephone/Facsimile: 01968 678 789
e-mail: acadcolr49@aol.com

Prologue

I have been asked many times why I am writing this book and what it is about. Sometimes this question is asked with interest, sometimes with a disapproving or dismissive look. These are simple enough questions to answer in theory, but in practice require mind and soul searching. Who am I? What have I done that warrants the writing of a book? What have I got to say that others might want to read?

'You want to know the future?' said the gypsy whom I met by 'chance'. Startled, I stared at her. 'You've known since you were a child what you would do one day. Write the book,' she said, and with that dismissed me. Long forgotten now, but suddenly re-awakened, were memories of poems and stories I had written as a child, which had enabled me to escape from the troubles of everyday life and given me a sense of peace.

Now, I laughed with joy at the idea of this book. For several years I had been writing on all sorts of different subjects and had often wondered what I would do with the information. What was it all for? Now I had a clearer picture. This book describes the awakening of my soul, tracing its origin and illuminating the patterns and conditioning that held me back from being in my true essence. It is a journey of miracles and personal transformation.

This book has opened a door to my own personal truth. I would like it if it inspired you to open a door to your own personal truth. It is the road of 'Let go, and let God.'

When you begin to look inwards
Your soul begins to look outwards

Part One

Stormy Beginnings

Chapter One

I am walking along Kingsburgh Road to the house that I lived in for so many years. I feel very different because for the first time I have the keys and I am alone. As I get closer, the house seems enormous. It is on the end of the terrace and right outside I see the laburnum tree blossoming bright yellow, its petals scattered on the path. I turn the long silver key in the lock and push open the huge black door. Inside the porch is another door, its stained glass an intricate arrangement of shapes and colours. I pull the front door shut behind me. There's a slam. It's as if I can hear for the first time.

The first thing I notice is the silence. I look around the porch and see things that had escaped my notice until now: the hall cupboard with all the coats hanging up, the polished table with its lamp. As I move into the main hall I'm aware of the soft powder-blue carpet flowing out to all the rooms. I can see now the beauty in these things that have been no more than objects before, and it's with excitement that I realise I can freely enter any of the rooms at will. I wonder which one to choose first.

As I move deeper into the house, the stairs lie in front of me carpeted in green, with yellow flecks. Sometimes I dislike this colour, but today it looks different, almost beckoning me. I decide to go up these stairs I have so often cleaned: hoovering the carpet, polishing the wood, dusting the banisters and shining the brass rods. As I climb I continue to be struck by the silence of the house. There's simply no sound.

I start with the door that's usually kept closed and only ever opened for special occasions such as parties or Christmas. It's where I had my weekly piano lessons. Now as I look around this room, the first thing I notice is the craftsmanship of my father in the alcove he made which rounds off a corner of the room. It seems only natural to me that the room should be softened by the curve of the alcove. I switch on a light that illuminates the shelves and see the ornaments. I pick them up and turn them over in my hands – carved ivories of elephants and other animals, some black, some cream, that my great-aunt brought back from Kenya where she was a nurse. Animals were killed for this. I put them back carefully.

The silence in the room is almost overpowering. I think about the many Christmases in here, the tree standing proudly in the window, my father's hand-made decorations of Santa Claus and his reindeers, all cut out of cardboard and painted, hanging round the walls. There would be letters spelling out 'Merry Christmas' in Gaelic, because my father had begun to learn the language. I would be hiding behind the sofa, 'seen and not heard', excitedly guzzling sweets – especially the Newberry Fruits – that had been given as presents.

I notice the record player, still there, on which I would listen to the singles I used to get as presents. Marmalade's 'Obladi, Oblada', and 'Sugar Sugar' by the Archies, to which I made up dance routines. And the chairs where people would sit, laughing and joking, having fun. I can almost smell mince pies and Christmas pudding permeating the house. Christmas Day was such a drama. It required weeks and weeks of preparation. Memories of the carol singers outside flit across my mind's eye, and I remember my first transistor radio, my birthday parties held in this room and the windows that are low and look out onto the street. And it's as if I can still see the neighbour across the road in her window looking over, watching me swinging on my curtains at night, then phoning my mother to tell her I am out of bed yet again. I turn around and remember the room is empty, silent.

I walk into the landing and a thought strikes me: I have rarely been allowed into my parents' bedroom, apart from occasionally taking in a breakfast tray. I wonder what secrets are in here. The room must hold some history, some information about my mother, about her past. It must reveal something to me. I open the door and am surprised it is so plain. The walls are cream. It's a very ordinary room. There's a mahogany wardrobe, a chest of drawers and a double bed with a headboard which Dad made with units at either side. On Mum's side there's an orange clock, also made by my father.

I cross to the window and look out across and down to the window of my bedroom and imagine Mum standing here gazing out. What does she see when she stares across at me? What is it she wants to see? Or what is it I have to hide? I used to keep my curtains closed to escape her prying eyes. Looking around my parents' bedroom, I'm confused because there's nothing that tells me anything new about her. I was so sure it held secrets.

I leave the bedroom and pause at the spare room. The door is shut. I don't like this room because I feel there's a presence in it. Both my granny and my great-aunt had stayed in it. No one had actually died there, yet that's what I feel. I also have memories of sometimes being shut in this room as a punishment. I don't like it. I'm not going to go in.

Next door is the bathroom. I remember my mother locking herself in, telling me she was going back to live with Granny if I didn't want her. And I was sitting on the other side of the door on the floor, screaming and crying, begging for her to come out because I couldn't reach the light switch and the house was dark.

The bathroom is an odd, strangely shaped room. My dad did a lot of work on it. One day when I was sitting there a figure appeared. At first I didn't believe it but I wasn't scared. It was a grey shape, an image of a man. There were no words spoken between us and yet I could hear what he was saying. I pinched myself repeatedly because I knew this couldn't be real. He said he had been 'sent' as a messenger of God and that one day I would recall this incident and everything would fall into place, and that although I was very lost at the moment, I was special. After he disappeared I felt as if I had been embraced by a wonderful loving energy and that the rest of my life would hold the moment of that day in the bathroom.

Further along is my bedroom, my first bedroom in this house, which looked out over the street. When I was young I would look out at the dark indigo sky and see the stars, wishing I could go home. I used to swing on the curtains and talk to the stars, as if they understood, as if this earth wasn't my real home. The yellow furniture and orange handles that Dad had made, the walls splashed with yellow, the single bed, are all still here. I remember hearing footsteps walking up the stairs and my calling out, believing it was my mother or my father, but there was nobody there. Eventually I accepted there was no one there and buried my head under the covers.

I leave my room with a feeling of peace and go back downstairs. The sun is shining through the stair window, its rays brightening the carpet, making it seem rather pretty now. I smile as I think, 'Well, the stairs won't get hoovered today, nor the brass polished. That's not going to happen for a long time.' And as I reach the bottom of the stairs I glance towards the small lounge which was made into a bedroom for Mum when she was ill. In it is a desk which is usually kept locked but now that she is in hospital I can open it. That's where the secrets are, letters and information about me that at odd times I've glimpsed and which I can now read at my leisure, with my feet up. Furthermore, with Dad on his own, we can talk and perhaps he will tell me all the things I still need to know about my past.

As I enter the lounge I notice that I'm still holding the keys of the front door in my hand. It dawns on me that it is my house now and how easily I can run it. I feel released from whatever has gone on in the past and realise that it doesn't matter any more – I don't even want to remember it. Now I've got the keys to the house I can use them to come and go. I'm sixteen, I've got my dad, I've got my dog and I don't have to watch out any more. I don't have to be clever or protect myself any more. This is my house. My space. And she's not here so I'm in charge. It's peaceful now and I can see the beauty here. I do love this house. It is part of me and I am part of it.

I feel great, uplifted. I know everything that will follow.

Dad will be home at his usual time, 5.25 p.m. on the dot. I have a new life of freedom.

I make straight for the desk. I'm not frightened of being caught because I know Dad won't be back for a few hours. I can take my time. For a moment I sit down without opening it. I allow my thoughts to go back in time, as if transported back to that awful day three years ago, when once before I had sat at this desk. I was thirteen years old.

I had been planning for months how I would get the chance to rummage through my father's desk. I was naturally curious. I had caught glimpses over his shoulder of a file with the word 'Alison' marked on the front. What was in it? I knew that my history was incomplete. I was never shown photos of myself as a baby, nor allowed to mention my birth. At last the moment came. My mother was out and I seized the opportunity. When I went to the desk, I found it unlocked. With hands trembling, I lifted the lid as if I were opening Pandora's box.

I saw the file with 'Alison' marked on the front. I opened it, and the first word that met my eyes in big bold letters was the word 'Adoption'. Disbelief. I re-read it and re-read it. It wouldn't sink in. You hear people say their stomach fell to the ground – well, that's what mine did. My head felt enormous, like it was going to explode as my mind tried to deal with all the questions. If I was adopted, my father wasn't my father. But my father *was* my father. I had always been told so. I knew my mother wasn't my mother, *that* I could remember, but *Dad, Dad*, I had always looked at Dad and thought, at least I'm his. I had some of his intelligence, some of his outlook and he could always answer my questions. And now to find out I didn't even belong to him, that I had no link to him, I felt my world collapsing. No mother, and now no father. I wanted to cry.

I'm sitting at the desk again. I am not rushed this time. I am free to search deeper. I want to know who I am. Who was my real mother? Once again I open the forbidden desk. Once again, I see the file marked 'Alison'; once again, I look inside and find the papers marked 'Adoption'. But, this time, it's no surprise. I take my time. I read the letters saying what a beautiful baby I was. I look more carefully at my birth certificate. It gives my birth mother's surname as Porteous, a name I have never heard before. And my father? My birth father, it simply states, was unknown. I still didn't know who I was.

Chapter Two

My life began in 1955. My incarnation had been planned with precision. Time, 4.04 a.m.; date, 27 May; place, Edinburgh.

From the very beginning I felt part of the stars, the galaxies, the universe, bathed in a wondrous indigo. When I meditate now I can go back to this beautiful place at will where anything and everything is possible. To float and fly in that solar system is my salvation, my true home. It's like the film *ET* when all he wants to do is go home. That feeling made a great deal of sense to me.

Then out of the indigo I experienced the sound of unfamiliar noises, different sensations, different feelings: a strong pull and an awareness of something else, another being, pulsating loud and clear. Where am I? Feelings of hurt, pain, frustration and despair bombard my soul. They are not my feelings. Who is this person I am curled up inside? I hurt. Somehow I've used this person to give me physical life and yet why, when I need peace and tranquillity? I want to go back to my indigo home. I am cold and my heart is heavy. I know I am doomed. The noises are very loud, sharp and penetrating, as if piercing me. It's unbearable and seems to go on forever.

On my mother's part, my birth went well. She was glad it was all over so she could get back to normal. I could feel her love for me but behind her eyes she seemed to be saying goodbye. I knew then we were not going to be together for long and the tears in her eyes confirmed my fears. She left me behind and before long I was moved to a different place. Suddenly I am apart from her and alone, not knowing where I am. I hear sounds similar to my own – crying, sobbing and screaming, which frighten me and cut through me as I lie in my cot for days on end, week after week.

When I was four months old a couple came to see me. It felt strange but comforting to be lifted out of my cot, to be held and talked to: up until then I had only been lifted up to be changed or fed. The couple were called Charles and Maude and they often came to hold me. I looked forward to their visits. Somehow I knew when they were coming and feelings of excitement would well up inside me. I'm sure they didn't realise that even very small babies are capable of picking up and understanding emotions and feelings, but I 'knew' these people were of great importance to me. I was told they were to be my father and mother and later on they spent hours trying to get me to say 'dad' and 'mum'. I thought this was fun, and it gave me feelings of joy and happiness. The woman called 'mum' was strange and I wasn't sure how she felt since she wasn't able to show her emotions, to let go and love. The man's feelings I was sure of and I would sit and stare at him peacefully. I knew he loved me.

I was adopted when I was six months old and 'Mum' and 'Dad' came to pick me up to take me to 'Applegarth', my new home. I never went back to the cot nor to the people I had begun to get used to. Within my first six months, I had had two mothers and three homes.

With my new mum and dad, life evened out for a while. I was the centre of attention for lots of people, especially my grandfather, my mother's father, and a woman called Brenda. They 'gooed' and 'gahed' and made funny noises at me, picking me up, poking and prodding me, putting me down and passing me around, while my dad was usually in the background casting a watchful eye. My mother, always withdrawn, never took much interest in me. She did, however, knit lovely clothes and make sure that I was always well dressed, but she wasn't able to give me the depth of love and affection I needed. Everyone used to comment on what a lovely, well-dressed little girl I was and how beautifully she had made my clothes, but I wonder if anyone really saw me, or if they only saw the clothes.

Suddenly I was uprooted again from my garden sanctuary of apple trees. We moved to a modern bungalow in Warriston and 'Applegarth' was a home of the past. Gradually I began to recognize the routine of daily life and I would know, for instance, when my dad was coming back from work. I would wait at the window every night, a good half hour before he was due to come home, and when his car drew up, I would run down the path to greet him. A little girl with blonde curls, a large smile and an energetic skip, running with outstretched arms to embrace her father. This picture was confirmed to me many years later when I married my first husband: his aunt had lived next door to us and she remembered the little girl waiting at the window for her daddy to come home. Life remained relatively calm until one day Mum chose to end it all.

I was four years old. The morning started out as any other. I thought we were having a big party because of the huge amounts of food that were being delivered. It was very exciting and Mum busied herself in the kitchen, cooking and preparing. I was ushered out and couldn't understand why she wouldn't even look at me and wouldn't come near me. Lunch consisted of nibbles from the food she was preparing and I remember feeling very hungry, but it seemed as if she was in her own world and that I didn't exist.

Later on in the afternoon, she locked me in the lounge and told me to look out for my dad coming home. I waited and waited. I was cold. I cried and cried, but to no avail. I was scared. All the feelings of abandonment at birth flooded over me. I called but there was no reply. Again and again I cried into the emptiness. I tried the door. It wouldn't open. I tried the window to see if I could open it, but I couldn't. I wasn't tall enough. I tried to reach for the light switch. I couldn't. I wasn't tall enough. I was cold; I was hungry. I was lost and frightened and I needed my dad. And what was wrong with Mum? Where were all the people for the party? Why couldn't I hear Mum? Why didn't she hear me? Then there was darkness, and through my tears I saw the stars twinkling their comforting light.

I heard a car. At last, it was Dad, but I couldn't run out to meet him. He saw me from the window and saw my despair.

His face was screwed up in a puzzled frown, wondering why I was standing at the window without the lights on. Why was I crying? He was taking it all in. A chain smoker of sixty a day, with a cigarette in his hand, he looked at me, silently questioning why I was not running out to meet him. He saw my fear-creased face. Time stood still. He threw away the cigarette and opened the front door. However, he didn't come straight in to see me and I was left wondering where he was and what he was doing. I banged on the door; I knew he was there, but what had happened to him when he entered the house? I banged my fists on the door again, but still no father. At last the door opened. I stepped back. He frightened me. He looked grey and sad, withdrawn, and there was a funny smell. I suddenly lost my hunger and began to shake. I felt so cold, as if I had been outside in the snow. At last the lights went on. Dad walked past me and opened the windows. I began to shiver. I didn't understand what the smell was or why he had opened the windows when it was so cold.

My mother had gassed herself in the oven and died that afternoon. All the food she had prepared for my father and me, which would have lasted us for at least two weeks, had to be thrown out because it was contaminated by the gas.

Hungry, cold and confused, I remember a woman arriving, a neighbour, and putting on a heater, one that blew air from the top. I was shaking so much that she told me to lift my skirt over it and I would soon warm up. I knew I wasn't usually allowed to do this, but she insisted. More and more people arrived, although nobody really paid much attention to me. I was left alone with strangers, wondering where Dad was, where Mum was and why I couldn't eat the food which I knew Mum had been preparing all day. What was happening? Then the police arrived; they were all dressed in black and I wasn't sure if I should fear them. What were they doing here? Nobody told me where my mum was and dread welled up inside me. I knew then that nothing would ever be the same again.

Eventually, I heard an ambulance arrive and I ran to the window. The ambulance men were in the house for just a short while and left carrying a stretcher with my mum on it, covered in a white cloth, not moving. I wanted to go out to see her but

I was dragged away from the window. Dad came in looking ill. I had never seen him without his smile before. He told me that Mum would not be coming home again; she had had a heart attack. My heart pounded; I felt sick. It was the sickness of contamination. Everything changed that day. From the moment the delivery van arrived with the food, my thoughts had been of joy and happiness at the promise of a party. Now I knew never to trust the promise of happiness, of a bright day dawning. All my feelings of hurt and pain returned. My day, my reality would always turn out differently. I could not depend on anyone or anything, for if I did I would always be left alone.

The days that followed were confused and hazy. People arrived and disappeared. Everyone seemed to be very sad and nobody would look at me straight in the eye. I missed my mum. I wondered where she was. Dad tried his best but he looked ill and I worried about him. I felt sorry for him. He had changed; he wasn't the same any more. Although he was around the house all day, there was a distance between us and I wondered if he was going to die and leave me as well.

Many different women came to the house to talk to my dad about looking after me as he had to go back to work. I didn't want him to go back to work because I was frightened that every time he left I would never see him again. My thoughts about the women who came to look after me were not pleasant ones either. I didn't want anyone else to care for me; it was my house and these were my things; he was my father. I was protective of the only things I had left. They were outsiders and I didn't want them here. I knew that no one could care for me like my mother had and I felt lost. I had no mother and no love, just strangers to look after me. I objected to their attempts to tame me. I was wild.

Strange as it seemed to most people, Mum still visited me every night or in the morning. She would appear, sitting on the golden quilt on my bed, and although she never actually spoke, I could see and hear her clearly. Nobody believed me and I found this odd: if I could see her so clearly, why couldn't they? Mum's 'visitations' really disturbed Dad so he decided we couldn't live in the same house any longer. I was now not allowed to mention

Mum's name and all photographs of her were removed. I was extremely distressed. My whole life was to be uprooted yet again. I thought that if we moved house I would lose my mother for ever, that she would no longer know where to visit and I sulked and yelled and screamed, but Dad was adamant that it wasn't healthy for me to 'see' my mother. We would have to move.

It is only in recent years that I have been able to remember details of Maude's death. I had buried it so deep inside me. Traumatic events, when they happen early enough in life, can leave a permanent scar – just as when a young heifer or bullock is branded with its owner's stamp, the mark stays for life. My mother's death shaped the way I saw the world for many, many years to come.

I can now look back on that time with greater understanding as if it happened to another me or another person. At the age of four my way of coping with the trauma was to ask questions to which no one gave me satisfactory answers. I would be told my mother had died and that was that; we had to get on with life and put the past behind us. But even at four years old, I knew my father and the others weren't telling me the whole truth. I knew in my heart that truth is simple. What was the smell? Why couldn't I see Maude? Why couldn't I eat the food? I was told half-truths and lies but because I was so young and innocent, I didn't understand why I wasn't being told the truth; I just knew that I wasn't. Another part of me thought there must be a good reason for it, because I honestly believed that grown-ups knew the answer to everything. I started to feel shut out, as if an invisible wall had been put in place. And once this wall was in place, it was very difficult to pull it down again. I began to imagine that grown-ups couldn't be bothered with me which made me invent my own version of the 'truth' to fill the gap. I was left feeling different, lonely, always searching and feeling there must be more, but I didn't know what.

Inside I was very angry, especially when my friends ridiculed me for not having a mother. I would lash out at them and the thoughts in my head would hurt me. I was confused; I knew my mother wasn't coming back but I could still 'see' her. I was also angry with her because she had left me alone, she had left

Dad alone, she had hurt Dad. I felt she had hidden something from me. I didn't know it then, but with her death, it was as if a seed had been planted and one day I would have to turn over the soil and find out what was there.

I was told we were going to move again, this time because of Maude. My dad thought that if we moved, I wouldn't continue to 'see' her. I'm sure he felt he was protecting me. Looking back, I can see that Maude's death was my first true experience of spiritual denial from others. I didn't understand their fear, but I decided it must be bad to die and if you did, no one would want to see or speak to you. That was how my own fear of death and dying began.

Everything changed after that. Dad changed, the house changed, new people came to look after me and Dad began to go out with the woman called Brenda. I was angry at not having a mother, that Dad couldn't be there for me, that I was being told what to do by strangers who didn't really care about me. All my feelings of loss and hurt came out as rage, and were mostly directed at one person.

Chapter Three

We moved from our bungalow to a ground floor flat round the corner and Mum came too. She still appeared to me at night or in the morning until I began to be unsure if this was a bad thing, so little by little I tried hard not to see her.

I continued to play with the children who lived locally. They picked on me and teased me, telling me I was different. 'You have no mother,' they would shout, repeating it over and over again. 'You're different,' they would cry, 'No mother!' over and over, day in, day out. This went on until one day a little girl said it once too often and I picked up a brick and threw it at her with all my might. Suddenly all the doors were closed to me. Children and parents were frightened. I had ostracised myself by showing my temper. From then on it all went inward. One of the children did eventually speak to me and I allowed her to push me down a flight of stairs so that she would be my friend: I learnt that I could bargain for friendship.

I even used my bruises to bargain for my father's love. I couldn't sit down because my bottom was so sore and Dad, seeing I was upset, tried to comfort me. Through my tears I asked Dad if I could scribble on my story book, something I knew was strictly forbidden. Dad had principles about books: you never wrote on a book, they were to be respected, and I wanted him to break that principle to prove to me how much he loved me. The unthinkable happened. He let me do it. The tears dried up instantly, my sore bottom forgotten. I had a ball, scribbling on every page and then ripping the book to shreds, page by page. It gave me a feeling of power and release. I began to learn the art of manipulation. If you make a big enough fuss, you'll get your own way.

But there was a lot more to this incident than simple childhood manipulation and testing of boundaries. I had an extraordinary memory and knew that I could memorise a story after having heard it only once. It was just like a film I had seen where a robot could put its finger on a page and instantly zap the information into its memory. I could do that, I could memorise stories instantly. By destroying my story book I was trying to get my father to understand this about me, to see me for what I really was, to see how I was different. To me he was a great person who knew the answers to everything. He was my teacher and I was asking him for his input. Destroying the book was my way of saying, 'Talk to me, don't give me books. Teach me your wisdom.' I was an old soul in a child's body, trying to reach my father on a soul-to-soul level, asking him for knowledge. I was crying out for spiritual wisdom and teaching. It was difficult to bridge the gap between the old soul and the young body and I wanted my father to help me.

I knew I was different, and being teased for having no mother was just a convenient tag. I was always perceived as the child who was unpredictable and, looking back, I was, in a way. I used to go off and do things on my own and it was about this time that I started to see bright luminous colours. They were like triangles of glowing colour, brighter than I had ever seen. I called them my fairy colours and I used to watch them, fascinated. They gave me a peace that was to remain with me for a large part of my childhood: I could tell them of my fears and my pain and silently they would heal me with their colours; they'd move into me and inflame me with wondrous love, accepting everything about me, loving me just as I was. So on one level I never felt lonely. I always talked and laughed with my fairy colours even when there was apparently no one there.

I often wandered around outside on my own. I looked like a street urchin because my clothes would get dirty within minutes of going outside. I remember one day the men were tarring the road and my dad forbade me to go near the huge pile of tar. I couldn't resist, however. I had to feel it, I had to go in it to experience it, and I was covered. The tar got everywhere, on my hands, in my hair, on my clothes. I rolled in it. Everyone was appalled. I couldn't stand still. I loved getting all this attention. I felt elated, while the grown-ups were expressing exactly the opposite. It took hours to scrub the tar off and my dad was nearly crying because he had to cut all my hair.

And I remember another incident. I spied a rocking horse through the window of one of the houses in our street. I knocked on their door and asked them if I could ride it and they let me. I could see our house from their window and I used to rock wildly on the horse while I looked down on the street and watched people searching for me. It was a game; 'How long would I let them search for me?' All they had to do was look that way and they would see me through the window. I felt as if I'd crossed over into another dimension: because they didn't see me I imagined I was in a different world. It was playful, but it was also very important that they should find me. Afterwards, I told Dad where I was and he didn't mind, so long as he knew.

The pattern of my going to the window every evening to look out for my dad continued. Nowadays he wasn't always back for his tea. My nannies scolded me for not being in bed but I didn't care what they said. My indigo home was far away, my father wasn't back, and my mother didn't visit me any more. The old soul inside the little body questioned. Who am I? Why am I here? Why this great loneliness?

I was five years old when my father began to go out with Brenda, who many years later I discovered had been Maude's bridesmaid. They would go out most evenings while I was left at home with various different baby-sitters. They probably didn't go out that often, but it certainly felt like it when I hadn't seen Dad all day and in the evenings he was out with Brenda. This compounded my sense of abandonment and I hated this woman for it. It was she who became the focus of my anger.

Brenda soon began to come to our house for lunch. It seemed to me as if she was trying to take over, to take Maude's place; and I resented her for it. She didn't have very much to say to me and my father wasn't the father I knew before, the one who used to spend time with me and talk to me. We also began to go to her home where she lived with her mother and brother.

Here I met a world of fresh people. Brenda's mother was kind and caring, but I still felt like an outsider. I disliked being there, supposedly on my best behaviour, to be seen and not heard. Their conversation was only for themselves. I learned to live how they wanted me to, disliking myself for my weakness. But the moment their backs were turned I would get up to some mischief.

Brenda's brother was a dentist, a perfectionist by nature with an eye for anything that had been touched or moved. I was the type of child who couldn't resist picking things up when no one was looking. I remember my uncle had a round wooden Solitaire board with coloured glass marbles, which fascinated me. I would pick them up and stare into them, seeing all the different coloured shapes inside. Swirls and twists and specks. I was like a gypsy looking into a crystal ball. I would put them in order of colours and there would always be a 'bad' one. This was the one I liked least. I played a game where the bad marble could be redeemed by being surrounded by the good marbles. I would fire it into the ring of marbles on the floor and if it rolled too far, it was still bad. If it stopped inside the ring, it was redeemed. Sometimes the bad marble pushed a good one out, and this became the new bad marble. Some marbles, though, the colours I liked best, could never be bad. I could sit for hours playing with the marbles. To me they were alive. After playing my game, or if I thought someone was coming, I would quickly gather them up and place them back on the board as if I had never touched them. Sometimes one rolled under the chair and I had to find it, terrified of losing it and being caught.

Dad took me to Brenda's house more and more often while they went off on outings together, or at other times I was sent to the house of the woman who looked after me during the day. Her house was very different to Brenda's. It was a third floor flat in a tenement block. I liked the flat. It was small and homely, and although it didn't have much, it was warmed by a lovely coal fire which I would watch until my eyelids closed for the night. The woman was large and cuddly. She showed me great kindness and I felt at one with her, as if this home were somewhere I could truly belong.

But these days were short lived. My father and Brenda soon announced their forthcoming marriage and her role, I was told, was now to be that of my mother. I was in a state of utter disbelief. She could never be my mother.

The wedding day was set and the honeymoon arranged, and my disbelief continued unabated as the 'happy' day approached. My head hung low. Why was I the only one who hated this day? I'm sure everyone saw me as a troublesome child – I was so unhappy that even the party didn't excite me. I knew my father wouldn't go away on honeymoon and leave me. I just knew he wouldn't do that. My belief in him was so strong that nothing and no one could convince me otherwise. The weather was dreadful. Storms and thunder with torrential rain made me certain that my prayers had been answered and my father would stay. My eyes hardly left him all evening as I constantly identified his form amongst the dresses and trousers of the wedding guests. At nine o'clock that evening, when almost everybody had left, he and his new wife were standing in the large hall saying goodbye. I screamed, I ranted and raved. I cried. I was told I was being ridiculous. I was told I was being selfish, but it made no difference. He was leaving. No one understood my feelings. They told me it would soon pass, that it was only two weeks, after all – although to a child it seemed like a lifetime. They told me it would be all right, and that I should be ashamed not to let them go. I remember how I had to be prised away from my father as he left and the last pleading look I gave him, as he stood beside this tall, thin woman at the far end of the hall.

They went and I stayed. For two weeks I lived in Brenda's house with Brenda's mother, my new grandmother, and her brother, my new uncle.

Chapter Four

When my father and Brenda returned from their honeymoon we moved into a new house in Kingsburgh Road. It was a large and spacious end-of-terrace building with back and front gardens and the number five on the door. The space frightened me and the rooms, with their high ceilings, usually had their doors shut. Here was another move; another house to get used to, miles away from where we had lived before; another foundation broken, or so I thought. As it turned out, Kingsburgh Road was to be my home for the next 12 years.

In our last house we had lived close to my grandfather, Maude's father, whom I loved dearly. I had been used to visiting him every day and spending a lot of time with him. I couldn't do this any more once we had moved; he had to come to us. One day, I was at my bedroom window and I was over-joyed to see my grandfather coming up the path. I was just about to run downstairs and throw myself into his arms, when my joy turned to confusion. I saw him turn away and walk back down the path. I was devastated. Dad and Brenda had turned him away at the doorstep. I wanted to run after him, hug him and feel the love he gave me. I couldn't understand why I wasn't allowed to see him. The only thing that was said to me at the time was that he was causing trouble and would try to turn me against my father, but I knew I loved my father so how could that be? After this a sadness set in. Every night I would play with the basket he had brought me, and pray that I would see him again. I never did. He never came back. I was broken-hearted and I am sure he was too.

My new mother and I settled down to an uncomfortable relationship. Sometimes it became so unbearable that she put a physical barrier between us. She would punish me by shutting me in the spare bedroom of which I had told her I was extremely frightened. Left alone there, I felt the fear in the back of my legs, and my breathing became difficult. I needed to get out of the room and no matter how much I screamed, kicked or ranted, nobody came. Hysteria would overwhelm me until at last my mother would let me out, telling me to wash my face and hands before my father came home from work.

Looking back, any chance of this relationship working verged on zero. In her role as my new mother she began to tell me what to do and I hated her for that. Almost as soon as Maude died, Brenda moved in. From my five-year-old point of view, it was as if she had taken Maude's place and maybe that was the reason Maude died. We could never have got on because whatever she was like, I would have resented her. I even resented her the first time she came for lunch and told her she shouldn't talk with her mouth full. She couldn't handle me. It was a confusing time, too, since Maude was still visiting me at night, but when Brenda constantly reappeared, I eventually had to accept that she was going to be a permanent fixture.

There was a lot of jealousy on both sides: we both wanted my father's affection. I found her cold and indifferent. If she tried to show me affection, I couldn't accept it. I would stand rigid. I didn't know whether I wanted her as a mother or not – sometimes I did, sometimes I didn't, but I knew I wanted a mother. If my cousins came through from Glasgow and she took their hand I didn't like it. I felt jealous. I didn't really want her, but at the same time I didn't want anyone else to have her either. I couldn't understand it.

I spent much of my time on my own but I always had my fairy colours to comfort me. They brought me peace, fun, silent communication and many, many different energies. I trusted and looked out for them. At night they played and danced around the room, laughing and having fun. When I was sharing a room with Brenda one night before she and my father got married, she read me a story. I, meantime, was curled up trying to stifle my laughter because the fairies were playing games, trying to pull her hair for fun. During the day I saw them around people, as if they were both part of the person and yet detached. I could tell quite a lot about people by the fairy colours around them and I became the silent observer, chastised many times for apparently staring and dreaming. The colours gave me information about the person's moods, feelings and physical state. I could 'feel' the person with a knowing and sometimes even predict their future. I would often have tea parties with my fairy colours during which we would talk and laugh and then everything in my life seemed to make sense. The colours were my peace and joy.

When I hated my mother I told her so. I told her I wished she would go away. That's when she would lock herself in the bathroom and tell me that she would leave and live with her mother again if I didn't want her. As darkness fell I became frightened. I couldn't reach the light switches and my mother refused to come out of the bathroom. Eventually I would huddle up close to the door, crying and saying I was sorry and that I loved her, begging her to come out. I hated myself for having to beg her to stay and yet another part of me wanted her. It was good having cuddles – brief, our arms around each other – but afterwards it didn't feel so good. I would hang my head and wonder if it was all worth it for a cuddle. When my father got home she passed the incident off as insignificant and completely missed out all the facts that had led to my becoming hysterical. She just shrugged and said I was a difficult child.

We were playing out a love triangle: my mother and I both determined to have Dad's love and Dad stuck in the middle. Triangles don't work but we continued to wrestle with it, sometimes seeking each other's love, but mostly vying for my dad's.

After a telling off and feelings of loneliness, I relied on my fairy colours the most. They helped me through the difficult times. I had two worlds. I also had my special 'friend', a Mrs Rose, whom I alone could see and who was clearly in another dimension. It was a great bewilderment to me why no one else could see her.

One time when we were on holiday at Loch Rannoch I

invited my mother to join Mrs Rose and me for a cup of tea. I had the tea set laid out and I pointed out to Mum where Mrs Rose was. I poured the tea and we all chatted. It was as if Mum could see Mrs Rose too. Although she said it was a pretend tea party with a pretend friend, it didn't matter; I knew Mrs Rose was actually there and we still had fun. I drank my tea with my pinky extended, making funny faces and laughing, pretending to be an adult, and so did Mum. Together Mrs Rose and I had many tea parties and many talks, and they allowed me to be in touch with my old soul without being dismissed as having childish imaginings.

Our pet labrador, Shuna, was my other confidant. She was extremely naughty and I loved her. My job was to walk her every morning which I enjoyed, but she was very strong and could easily pull me in any way she wanted to. Shuna was my true friend and so very funny. One day, not long after we bought her, she decided to chew through the telephone wires in the kitchen, and left us with no phone. When the engineer came out, Shuna disliked him immensely and barked loudly until he left, much to his annoyance. About a week later, however, Shuna repeated the process and chewed through the same telephone wires and the same engineer came back and proceeded to re-wire the phone. Having finished in the kitchen, the engineer then went upstairs to check the bedroom phone was working properly and by the time he came down, Shuna had already chewed through his replacement wires. He was outraged. I rolled around on the floor holding my sides with laughter but poor Shuna was sent to her bed. I knew just how she felt, lying there with her head on her paws, her eyes pleading forgiveness, following everyone's movements. She was in the dog house. I could really identify with Shuna's behaviour. How I would have liked to chew through the cords which tied me to the adult world! Shuna remained my friend and confidant throughout the following years.

Another important animal in my life at that time was Patsy. She was a stray we found while on holiday in Aviemore where we went every summer. One day, while out walking, I saw a tiny kitten mewing. She was scared and on her own. I picked her up and took her away with me. She was wild and vicious and Dad insisted that I take her to the police station. I was dying to keep her and the policeman said she was a wild stray so that I could certainly keep her. Dad wasn't so sure but, thank goodness, to my surprise, Mum said I could keep her and the kitten stayed. We called her Patsy. She was jet black with the most beautiful eyes and a mind of her own. I kept her in the garage because she was so vicious, but I somehow knew I could reach her and tame her. Slowly she began to trust. I would sit and watch her for hours, waiting for her to make a move towards me, and little by little she did. Then I introduced her to the house, to Dad and Mum and Shuna.

When we returned to Edinburgh, Patsy settled down but I could still see in her the hurt and pain that mirrored my own. She had been abandoned and didn't have a mother, and that attracted me to her. I mothered her. I thought, 'I'll tame her, I'll show my mother I can tame her.' But I never completely tamed Patsy. You could always see the wild stripes beneath her black coat, and she kept that bit of wildness in her nature. I really admired the fact that she wasn't taken in by our petting. She came and went as she pleased and I wished I had more of her independence.

For a period of time I wanted Patsy to love me only. It was a selfish love, and somewhere along the line I realised this was not a true love. I had to let her go, let her be, free to love as she wished. In that letting go, Patsy loved me more. The old soul in me was recognising the difference between control and freedom, dependency and independence.

Shuna was delighted there was someone she could chase and play with. Patsy agreed and used to wait for Shuna to pass by, then she would pounce on her and swing from her tail. Shuna would chase her all over the place. They became the best of friends and it was beautiful to see them together. Patsy believed that Shuna was her mother and they slept curled up in a big basket. These were my two best friends.

Chapter Five

I began school when I was four-and-a-half years old. It was a private school owned by two very old sisters in the centre of Edinburgh, called St. Serf's. Our classes were small and the buildings in need of repair. The gym and sewing rooms were across the tarmac playground and the most important room, the tuck shop, was in the basement.

School, through my eyes, was strange. I was one of those children who was always in trouble. There were two categories of children: the ones that were frumpy, strait-laced, academic swots; and the others who were not so academic, more out-going, fun-loving, creative. And then there was me! Wild and free. I would look at the other children in my class and try to copy their mannerisms, but it didn't matter how hard I tried. I still didn't seem to make a good impression. Black marks appeared as if by magic on the wall chart.

I was clumsy and dropped things; I was noisy and loud so that if anyone laughed in the class I could be heard above the rest and became the focus of attention. I also fidgeted all the time, my mind was always racing and I wanted to know everything, asking questions at times when I should have been listening. I also had a lot of energy. Every teacher, no matter what class I was in, thought, justifiably, that I was over-active. Everything had to be done at a hundred miles an hour. I wrote very badly because I wrote so quickly. I read very quickly and missed out words, and as I got older I couldn't understand things like algebra – it just didn't register in my brain. However, all this energy made me very good at sport. It's what I excelled at.

Being different made it harder for me to keep friends. My way of getting friends was to make as much mischief as possible. Rather like Shuna and the telephone wires, I expected everyone to romp along beside me. Naturally this would get them into trouble too, and would end in their shunning me.

Moira was my first best friend, a closeness helped along by the fact that our parents were good friends. It was also a friendship based on rivalry and our fall-outs often involved the whole class. They would start by siding with Moira, however I usually managed to turn the tables. It was somehow serious and playful at the same time. None of it was anything other than childhood rivalry because there was a great love between us: if somebody new came to the school we would both see if we could become friendly with them, then after a while we realised we'd missed each other and we got back together. I see this in my own children now with their friends – one minute they're speaking, the next they're not, and then it all blows over. We never lost touch and even now, you'd think we were sisters. We talk the same, we act almost the same and we look alike. We remained best friends for years and made a pact that when we were older and got married we would be each other's bridesmaid.

Friends sometimes asked me to their houses after school. I was not supposed to go but I went just the same, sauntering back home as and when I pleased. I knew I would be met by an angry mother who would punish me, usually sending me to bed with only a glass of milk for supper. I would be told to stay there until morning. I didn't mind all that much because alone in my room I could talk with Mrs Rose and see my fairy colours. It was a calm time to reflect on the day, so my mother's punishment did not work entirely the way she intended. I was happy to be on my own. The only down side was that I didn't get to spend time with my dad and felt excluded.

My mother wanted to impose a very strict discipline. Everything had to be just so. There was a time for everything. We ate certain foods on certain days, mince on Tuesdays and fish on Fridays. Her discipline was partly a reaction to my naturally wild and free-spirited temperament. My father was also a stickler for discipline: he had been in the army and was punctual to the minute, and his clothes were always neat and tidy.

But nothing could curb my wildness. I was like Patsy with her wild stripes beneath her dark coat.

Eventually my mother informed my friends' parents that I was not allowed to go visiting after school without her permission, which put paid to my roaming. This made it difficult for me to maintain relationships. I was only occasionally allowed to have friends at home and I became more and more of a loner, an outsider. When my friends played out late at night, I was pulled in. I had a curfew. Looking back, it really was a very disciplined upbringing.

From the age of six onwards I began to catch the bus home from school. At least I was *meant* to take the bus although most days I walked, usually very quickly so that nobody would know what I was up to. This enabled me to save my bus fares and spend the money on sweets. I really loved buying what I wanted because of the freedom it represented.

I made money by making clothes for trolls which I sold at school. I made them at night when I was meant to be sleeping, sitting up for hours in the dimming light, sewing little outfits in different materials for the girls at school to buy. I also did cartoon drawings of Mickey Mouse and other Disney characters and made them into posters to sell at school. They cost two shillings and sixpence, but five shillings if they were coloured in. I would draw these during school time. Certain teachers just turned a blind eye while others severely disciplined me. None of them picked up on the fact that I had a creative gift that could be developed. In fact the art teacher put me out of the class for being what she called 'too creative'. I wanted to allow my paintbrush or crayons to draw whatever came to me and express myself through colour, and I questioned why I had to draw what I was told to. In time, my imagination and sense of colour were stultified.

Once I was walking home alone. I was eight. A man jumped out on me and exposed himself, dragging me down a lane and forcing me to touch him. Somehow I managed to run away and kept running until I got to Granny's house which was the only obstacle on my secret journeys home. Usually I would run quickly past her house so that she didn't see me and tell my mother what I was up to. Now I didn't care if Granny saw me, I rang the bell and was taken in, crying, as I explained what had happened. Granny immediately called the police and then my mother. When the police arrived I became more frightened. They reminded me of another scene I had experienced. I had feelings of doom and flashes of memory which refused to become clear. I told the police what had happened, but my mother, agitated by the inconvenience and disgrace, proceeded to tell them that I had a very good imagination and it was probably all in my mind. The police were not so easily dismissed, however, and stated that it was a very accurate account. My mother replied, 'She always has to make a scene and embarrass everyone.'

My schooling at St Serf's continued until the fire department demanded that the two old sisters who owned it install a fire escape or close the school down. The school closed with the result that some of the parents and teachers became involved in raising money to buy an old house in Murrayfield, which they renovated and refurbished. This was to be our new school, to which I was proudly sent. Every weekend I helped my dad with tidying and cleaning, pulling out fireplaces or bagging up rubble. I was out of the house a good deal and spending time with my dad – altogether, it was a good time in my life.

I didn't really want to go to the new school in Murrayfield. Instead I wanted to go to our local council school where I might meet and play with the children who lived in the council houses nearby. But this wasn't acceptable to my parents. At the time I didn't really have much understanding of the importance my parents put on social standing. My father was a financial adviser and we lived in a private house, so they wanted me to mix with children of a similar background.

The new St Serf's was very small and in the middle of an upper-class district and we earned ourselves a reputation as St Trinians. We weren't 'proper ladies': we were loud, rebellious, noisy and we played football with our hats going down the road. Our parents had funded the place so there was an element of 'We own the school'. One time when it was really cold we brought in a thermometer, having already checked what the legal temperature of the school had to be. It was below the legal minimum so we walked out and nearly got expelled for it. We were always up to something. A new teacher came and said, 'Now, girls, I think we'll start a basketball team.' Within a week she had broken her arm; there was a fight and we were known to be rough.

We had another teacher who used to call us 'my girls' and she was a lovely lady, just like the Miss Jean Brodie character. She took us for shorthand and typing when we were older. We all clubbed together and bought the 'cheat's' book, the book with all the answers to the tests. In every other class we misbehaved, but Mrs Glen could be heard in the staff room saying, 'My girls are getting 80 per cent, 90 per cent in their tests every week.' Of course, when it came to our main exam we all got really low marks and she realised what we had been doing. I felt quite sorry for her because she had boosted us up to all the other teachers.

Some of the teachers turned a blind eye to my antics and there was one in particular who let me get away with murder. She took us for German, which I didn't enjoy, so I used to knit in the class instead. At first she would say, 'Alison, what are you doing?'

'Knitting, Miss,' was my reply. After a few weeks she stopped telling me off and started to ask, 'Alison, how is the knitting coming along?'

My mother always drilled into me the need for qualifications. One couldn't be anyone or achieve anything without them. They would allow me to do anything I wanted in life and always have something to fall back on, especially when I was older and received a good pension. This never felt right for me. I just wanted my freedom and to have fun.

Chapter Six

I was growing up, but not into the tame, domesticated creature my mother wanted. As I got older, I got braver in confronting her. We played a game of cat and mouse, switching roles, one provoking the other to confrontation. She would give me house-work to do: the brass to polish, the stairs to clean, the ironing to do; and I'd be more or less bribed into doing these chores or else there'd be no going out. Talking back or voicing a contrary opinion was out of order. Once I found an insect hiding in the salad when I got back late and I immediately assumed it had been planted there by my mother. Looking back, I realise that this was quite possibly paranoia. But whatever the truth, I became increasingly frightened of eating food that was served to me on my own.

One Saturday lunchtime we had herring in oatmeal and while my mother and father were enjoying theirs, mine tasted off and turned my stomach. When I complained, my mother said I was being ridiculous – theirs tasted fine and she insisted I eat it. I remained absolutely adamant until I became hysterical and, when my father could take no more, he decided to taste it himself. He was horrified to find it was indeed off. In my mind it was deliberate. Even then, I was punished for causing trouble and sent hungry to my room.

The game of playing cat and mouse sometimes ended in a physical fight. Dad seemed helpless to do anything about it, opting for a peaceful life rather than come between us. I was often accused by my mother of upsetting him and punished, but the punishment was nothing compared to the apologies my father asked me to make to my mother. I knew I was right, yet had to admit I was wrong. I hated that. I became quite determined to leave home as soon as I could.

When my mother and I fought, my father would shrug his shoulders in a helpless gesture and his face would be etched in pain. Seeing the pain and grief on Dad's face I felt guilty. I know that he was powerless to stick up for me and we were still in the triangle. Our natural feelings for each other dared not surface.

I became a recluse, escaping to my room, which was now a small room set over the back of the house.

Chapter Seven

I was 13 when the spirit appeared to me in the bathroom. I think many people have the idea that seeing spirits is a scary experience, but I wasn't scared at all because I was held within his energy, as if I were in another dimension which holds no fear. I believe spirits are made up of frequencies and we can enter their realm. When I saw the spirit I felt like I was in two realms at the same time, pinching myself to bring me back to 'reality'. When I saw the spirit everything else in the bathroom faded, and I was engulfed in this other frequency of energy in which all I could see was him. It was completely silent. I didn't find it strange that I could 'hear' what he was saying. He was a messenger of God and in an image I could relate to. He appeared to be like Jesus. He said that I had a special purpose in life and that one day I would remember this meeting. As I came back into the 'reality' of the room, the sun was streaming through the skylight window, its golden beams making me warm, uplifting me. I felt very special.

After this I began to see the colours around people more clearly. I could 'see' if they were ill; I could 'hear' if they were ill. I began to predict disasters, but for the most part I could see people's illness. I would sit on a park bench and watch passers-by, playing the game of what was wrong with them, my eyes instantly homing in to the area of their illness. Life soon became a wonderful world of colour and energy. Animals would come to me and I knew intuitively where their pain was and I would put my hands over the area. Once Shuna cut her paw badly on a slate and I was the only one there. I was terrified she would bleed to death. I knew I had to save her, and when I needed my fairy colours most they were there to tell me what to do. Following their guidance, I stopped the bleeding, bandaged the wound and managed to settle Shuna down. I got praise from my mother and father which made me feel great.

My great aunt Martha arrived back from Kenya and moved in with us. She was a medical sister; a small, thin, cantankerous woman who had suffered immensely throughout her life. After losing her husband and her unborn child, she became a recluse, living and working in Kenya, never to come home until now. We had a wonderful unspoken understanding; she inspired me and I identified with her hurt. She had a hardness about her which didn't frighten me because I understood how she felt. I could see her hurt and I could see that her hard exterior wasn't the reality. We would talk a great deal and she would tell me stories about nursing and healing. She liked me and had time for me, and I learnt a lot from her.

One night my parents went out, leaving me with Aunt Martha. That evening she seemed somewhat confused and I discovered she had taken too many sleeping pills. Intuitively, I 'heard' what to do and how to help her. I paced her up and down, making her walk and giving her plenty of water to drink. I kept talking to her and getting her to talk to me. I managed to bring the situation under control and knew instinctively that she would be all right, so I put her to bed and by the time my parents returned home she was sleeping peacefully. At first they didn't believe me; they listened vaguely and nodded, saying a few polite things, as I told them what had happened, but the next day Aunt Martha told the story and begged me to become a nurse. 'Nurses like you are God's gift to people,' she said.

'Hearing' and 'seeing' more clearly, I began to prophesy what would come about next. Aunt Martha eventually had to go into a nursing home and I believe she was past caring. I remember one Saturday morning the phone kept ringing, it stopped and then started again. I didn't answer it because I knew she was dead. Mum finally came through to answer the phone, and when she asked me why I hadn't, I replied, 'Because Aunt Martha is dead. That's the nursing home telling you.' She questioned me as to how I could possibly know that. The phone rang again. It was the nursing home. 'Martha is dead,' they told my mother. I realised that I 'knew' things before they happened, but other people obviously didn't because they seemed to find it strange, and this made me angry. I was also confused. To be given a gift and not be able to use it – what was the point?

Then my granny moved in with us, and my life became more difficult. I felt as if my mother now had an ally. Granny always left her denture gum in the bathroom, and this gum, according to my mother, was my chewing gum which I wasn't allowed to have. Time after time I told her that it wasn't mine, but she didn't believe me. One Saturday, while Dad was outside in the garden and I was in my room, my window open as it was a beautiful summer's day, my mother burst in unannounced, clutching the pink denture gum in her hand, yelling at me to admit that it was mine. I refused and a skirmish followed, and Dad, hearing the commotion, came into my room and pulled us apart. He demanded to know what was going on. I made my mother show him the pink substance, and he confirmed that it was indeed Granny's denture gum. My mother withdrew, mumbling some complaint or other and without an apology.

Dad shrugged, lowered his head in defeat and turned his back on me. He walked out of the room. I trashed my room, breaking my radio. I eventually calmed down and asked my father to mend it. But he refused, which shocked me. He said, 'You'll never forget this. This is what happens when your temper gets out of control. I will not mend your radio because you need to learn that it's not acceptable to vent your anger and smash up your belongings.'

I believed Dad's words and began to suppress my anger. In time, I became so full of negativity that there was no room for my fairy colours. I blocked them out. I wouldn't allow them to comfort me and eventually I lost touch with the spiritual world.

Chapter Eight

It was not long after the spirit appeared to me in the bathroom that I discovered my adoption. Discovering the truth about my past had a devastating effect on me. Adoption! Where did this leave me? Who was I? And who was Maude, whom I had always believed to be my mother? I could never understand until now why all my questions about her had been evaded. I was always told, 'The past is in the past – there's nothing you need to know, she died and that's the end of it.' Now that I understood why my questions weren't answered, it raised a new set of questions. Now I wanted to know who my real mother was.

The day after discovering the secret file I went to school confused and frightened; I blurted out my dark secret. I was looking at everyone and I knew they were looking back at me, but who was it they saw? I wasn't Alison. I had no reflection in the mirror, no one to identify with. It was all gone. They had a mother, a father, they had a home, they had their lives. If they were good at school work it was because they took after their mother or their father, if they had blond hair it was because one of their parents did.

I was in a dilemma. I needed to find out more but to ask my parents would be to admit that I had rummaged through their private desk. Eventually I plucked up my courage and challenged Dad. He drew the usual veil. 'I have no records, and what is past is past. I never knew your mother, I know nothing about her. It's better to let sleeping dogs lie.' Brenda told me I was wicked for having dug up the past and for hurting Dad and that I should drop it. He didn't want to be reminded of the past and I had no right to bring it up. It was making him ill. Her accusations were an inner torment to me because I would never do anything to hurt my father. She said I was insensitive and bad and I would end up like my real mother, 'a bad lot'. I wondered how she knew. I wanted to scream and hit them because I was sure they were lying.

I felt guilty for hurting my father and sad for the pain I could see in him, but I still needed to know the truth about my birth. I had no one to turn to. Feelings of helplessness and hopelessness swept over me. I didn't feel I belonged anywhere and I buried my pain very deep. One day, I vowed, I would find out the truth.

I wondered who I looked like, whose voice mine resembled, what my natural mother was like. And I began to have this fantasy about how wonderful she was and how much she loved me and how it must have been an awful tragedy that made her give me away. I created an image of her in my mind.

I think it was at that point that I determined to find my real mother. I just needed to wait until I was 16 when I would be able to trace her legally. I imagined that she would welcome me with open arms, that life would be fine and everything would work out and fall into place. I was convinced she was still alive and that somehow we had been unjustly parted: we were like Romeo and Juliet, meant for each other from the start. We would have an amazing love for each other, a real mother–daughter relationship.

This caused my relationship with Brenda to deteriorate further. I became fixated on the image I held of my natural mother and excluded Brenda from the picture, almost laughing and saying, 'Well, I know my real mother wouldn't do that, or would do that.' When I was bad she'd always say the same thing: that I'd turn out the same as my mother, a bad lot.

I wished my father would talk to me and open up to me. Knowing I wasn't his made me determined to try to be more like him. I read a book on radar because he had been a radar expert during the war. He worked as a financial advisor and I asked him to help me with arithmetic to prove to him I could add up figures too. I didn't let Brenda near my books or my work; I put up barriers. I did it deliberately, and Dad and I would work away together at nights while she would be on her own. By taking an interest in Dad's work and what he did, I gained more attention from him but it distanced me even further from Brenda.

It dawned on me now why I was so different. It was because I had no identity. I assumed that the whole world could see this too. My friends suddenly felt alien to me. They all had parents and an identity, but not me. I withdrew from them. I became sulky. I became angry, jealous and bitter of people who did have a family. I reacted badly to any comment – whether about school work, my looks, or my parents – ready to assume the worst possible interpretation. I became insecure and extremely defensive. I became a bully, ready to lash out at the slightest provocation. I wasn't an active bully, but a reactive one, cold and calm, ready to strike out at anyone who said anything against me. I didn't trust anyone, convinced they were all talking about me behind my back.

A lively, gregarious, energetic child; constantly questioning why; a real live wire; a Gemini turned into an awkward, silent, moody character, eyeing people with suspicion. I didn't feel I had much to offer.

School work wasn't important any more. My primary concern was urgent. Who am I *now*, not what will I be when I 'grow up'. My future wasn't of any concern. I didn't care to have a career, be married or have a family. I just needed to know, who am I?

Chapter Nine

I was 15 when James came into my life and I began to broaden my horizons. I met him ice skating and was immediately attracted to him. He was not only good looking but he was also a fine skater which I liked because I couldn't skate very well. He was 'acceptable': his mother taught at a college and my aunt had heard of him.

I had been brought up being told constantly that sex was dirty and bad, so I kept myself to myself and enjoyed a very platonic relationship with James. He was madly in love, and at the time so was I. Every Friday night we would go skating. I had to be home by ten o'clock and have all the housework done, but most Fridays I managed to get out.

James and I saw each other for almost a year and although we had no sexual involvement (not for want on his part), there was a closeness. I skived off school and went to his house where we played records and talked. I had found someone who truly cared about me.

One day Shuna ran away – she was in season – and my mother phoned the school to ask me to come home and find her. She discovered I wasn't there. I had always thought my mother could link into me telepathically, knowing what I was up to, just as I could link into her. I'd think, 'I wonder if she'll let me out on Friday night?' and 'know' if she was going to do something to stop me. 'She'll complain I've not polished the brass right or she'll create a situation where I'm going to lose my rag which means I'll be rude to her and give her an excuse for not letting me out.' I knew the scenario in advance. What I discovered on this occasion was that my mother *didn't* know I had been skiving off school until Shuna gave the game away. A new thought dawned on me. 'Mum does not know everything about me, I don't have to be as tied to her as I have let myself be. I don't have to obey her rules.'

When challenged about skiving off school, I belligerently denied it. Nothing would make me tell the truth. Then and there I began a new phase of life where I was going to stand up for myself and not take any more shit. I had discovered an urgent new strength. At school they couldn't touch me because I didn't care any more. Dad had given much of the money to finance the new St Serf's so I held this up as a ransom. They couldn't expel me because they still owed my father money. I became arrogant and took chances.

I was at an age where I could leave home. I felt I was now in control. In the lies and deceit was my freedom, and it was the beginning of a real hardness, a non-caring. I felt I didn't need these people, I didn't need anyone. I didn't give any of the teachers respect and they didn't respect me. Same with the prefects. Basically, you get back what you give out. Nobody gave a shit, because I didn't.

It was around the time the film *Easy Rider* came out and everybody had scooters or bikes. I loved to go on the motorbike of the boy who worked at the local garage, despite not being allowed out on bikes, or hang around boys, but George was accessible because I had to walk past the garage on the way to school. I would ride on the back of his bike, thrilling to the thrust of the engine. You could set your watch by the headmistress of our school – she was at the same place every day. I would meet George on his huge bike at the bottom of the road and wait for her car. As she appeared I'd shout, 'There she is, let's go!' and we'd scream up the inside lane, dodge in front of her car, just skimming the front bumper, and then screech away as the traffic lights changed, looking back and laughing. I felt as if I had become the bike, the charge was tremendous. She knew it was me, she would see the uniform and at school I'd get called into her office where I got a serious telling off. She'd also phone my mother but I didn't care. I loved it. I thought it was just great to be so out of control! At the age of 16, school was coming to an end and freedom was just around the corner.

I decided I would go to college to study child care as this seemed an easy option. You didn't have to have any particular O levels or Highers to do it, and to me, looking after children was something you didn't need a brain for. What could be difficult about it? I knew that if I went to college I would have my freedom. I could behave as I wanted to. No one could control me: I was an adult and I could do whatever I wanted. It wasn't as if I was going to have to actually learn anything, because what could you learn about kids? In reality I had no idea where I was going or what I was going to do. Escape was my one aim.

I had dreams. I always thought I would be famous. I thought I'd probably be a pop singer and someone would find me. It would be as simple as me walking down the street and someone catching a glimpse of me and saying, 'Yes, you're the next Cilla Black.' I often dreamt that I was leaving home and people would say, 'Oh yeah, and where are you going?', and I'd say, 'I'm going to London, I'm going to be famous, watch me. I'll make something of my life, and then you'll regret it. And then you'll say, oh, I wish I'd been nicer to her.' The reality was that I was just very lost and lived, to a degree, in a fantasy world of stardom, of what you see on TV. In the end, even I didn't believe in myself. I felt I had no qualities in my life and nobody saw anything in me. They didn't see that I could paint, nor that if I could sell my Mickey Mouse drawings, I must have a real business sense which could be cultivated.

I had an inner burning belief that I would stand out against the rest. I would go to London and I would take off, like Dick Whittington and his cat. Yet another part of me was scared. What if I ended up on the streets? Home offered me security, and I didn't quite dare live out my fantasy, or make it real in a get-away car. All this made me feel very confused. There was so much hardness setting in and so much determination, but no guidance. No one to say, Alison, you've got this talent, let's develop this side of you.

Instead of going to London, I made a short excursion across Edinburgh. I left Kingsburgh Road to stay with a friend whose father was an elder in our local church. He knew that I was experiencing difficulties at home and offered me a haven for a while. They had a pleasant house and were kind and caring. A peace came over me. The only thing was that I missed Shuna and Patsy.

Then James announced that he was leaving Edinburgh to move to St Andrews, a town 60 miles away, as he had been accepted at the university there. He told me we would stay together, but I had no delusions about our romance; there would be no fairy-tale ending. I knew that in time someone else would take my place, so I finished our relationship. I didn't want to be the one who got the letter saying that he had met someone else and feel that pain. My mother had always drilled it into me that there were plenty of fish in the sea and I adopted this attitude. Part of me also wanted the excitement of moving on, so I forced myself to forget James and turned my attention elsewhere. I needed a distraction.

I met David, a boy whom I was crazy about, and we started going out together. I was going to pubs and met David at my local. I was drawn to David's maturity, he was studying architecture and was much more grown up than James. He was attractive too, and didn't have a girlfriend, which made up all the right ingredients for me! I felt sorry for James when he sent me a letter with a huge red heart enclosed which had a broken bit, but I perceived that as a weakness. On the other hand, David's feelings weren't out in the open. I liked the challenge, I got a kick from drawing him into my net.

David wasn't in love with me until I'd finished with him because I discovered he had asked out another girl. A week later, I met him in the pub on his own and he declared his feelings for me. Too late. My lack of interest in him only fuelled his desire.

I had now discovered the power I had to control my relationships. I remember one evening in the pub. I had on a red top – in those days they were tight – and a short yellow skirt, when in walked the boy with whom I had always been in love, John. He used to deliver groceries to our house and he broke my heart when he began going out with my friend Tracy and not me. When he saw me, he was absolutely gob-smacked at how gorgeous I was. I was no longer this little girl with cropped hair, dressed in frumpy clothes, with what he called 'goldfish bowl' eyes. Now he thought my eyes were beautiful. I realised that if I could change the attitude of the one person I always wanted, if I had the power to get *him*, then I could get anyone. And that's when I began to understand what my mother had been saying about sex. That's what men wanted. I knew that if I'd slept with John that night I would never have seen him again, that I'd have been one of his many notches on the wall. After that, I used sex as a magnet to attract, but without giving it away.

I got a job in Wilkies, a clothes shop in the centre of Edinburgh, and began to earn some money.

I had opened the door to freedom. I had learned how to manipulate relationships. I was earning my own money. I could do what I wanted. But it was to take me another two decades to learn the true meaning of freedom.

Part Two

The Edge of Freedom

Chapter Ten

After just four weeks of living away from home, I was back; partly because I couldn't stay with my friend any longer and partly because Dad had pleaded with me to come home. At the time I thought my parents wanted me back so that they didn't have to explain to everyone why I wasn't living with them and make it obvious they couldn't control me. But in hindsight, I think it was a need. Like many couples whose children have flown the nest, they probably found an emptiness between them once I had gone. I think they really missed me and needed me to fill that gap, to keep in place the dynamic tension that held their relationship together.

Then Mum fell ill, coughing and coughing, and I could see it was no ordinary cough. For weeks I watched the life-force gradually slipping away from her, until one day I decided to call the doctor. He called an ambulance and when it arrived, dread welled up inside me although I couldn't understand why. Suddenly, I felt as if I was four again, watching Maude lying on the stretcher being taken to hospital, not Mum. Waves of panic swept through me as I struggled with these memories. Flashbacks of a forgotten past which I had buried deep inside.

I returned from hospital and for the first time, as I walked round the house in the silence, I discovered its beauty. I was seeing it in a new light. For me, being in charge of the house represented freedom. I was elated to be taking over Brenda's role. I could now do whatever I wanted. I could make whatever food I wanted; it didn't have to be mince on Tuesdays or fish on Fridays. I had wanted my freedom for so long. I used to walk along the street wearing high heels, pink sparkly ones like Cinderella shoes, complete with bag and make-up, trying to look like an adult. I think all children at some stage look for that maturity because it appears to them to open up doors to freedom.

With Mum in hospital, it felt as though I had my house and my dad back. I knew I could have time with Dad. He and I got into a routine for mealtimes, we did the shopping and cleaning together and I was in my element. Now the household chores were a pleasure. He took me to the pub on Saturdays. If Mum had known that she'd have had a fit. He would buy me a drink and proudly introduce me, saying, 'This is my daughter.' I loved it. I could use my intellect and be accepted, and Dad and I would talk, sometimes for hours, long into the evening. Or I could play my music full blast, or watch TV. He allowed me out in the evenings with my friends and trusted me to come home on time. We didn't argue and settled down to a very comfortable relationship.

My visits to the hospital to see Mum couldn't be short enough. I deliberately chose not to see the pain she was in. I had no feelings and no emotions. I simply felt numb.

Gradually, I saw the change in Dad. He was lost and lonely without Mum and began to drink heavily. At first I thought the drink was just part of the fun, but as the weeks passed into months, and Mum was still in hospital, getting weaker and weaker, there were more empty bottles of whisky and his speech was often slurred. I didn't want to think too much about what this meant. I had no idea how to help him cope with his pain.

I came home one day full of the usual happy feelings at the prospect of our ritual evening chat but as I entered the hall, my instincts went on red alert. I stopped abruptly. In front of me on the hall table, lit by the soft glow of the lamp, were photographs all spread out. I moved closer, curiosity taking over; spellbound, I began to pick them up and stare at the faces before me. The black and white snapshots were obviously of me and my guess was that the woman holding or playing with me had to be Maude. There was a much younger version of Dad – how striking he looked with his blond hair, tall and smiling! Memories tried to come, but to no avail. I couldn't remember this woman. I picked up one of the photos of myself and stared at it, taking in all the details, amazed that for the first time, I had in my hands a piece of my past. Why had I not seen these before, I wondered. But then how could I when they had been so well hidden? All the evidence of my life between the years of my birth to the age of five had been denied me. Now here it was, in black and white.

The house was silent. Alarm bells began to ring. Where was Dad? Holding my breath I cautiously pushed open the lounge door, not daring to imagine what I might see. There was Dad, slumped in his chair, drunk. He pulled himself up. There was no familiar warm greeting and I hardly recognised him. Something stirred in me. I had seen him look like this before, but when? I wracked my brain. He turned his eyes to me and uttered, 'Um, I must empty my heart to you and tell you the truth. Maude didn't die of a heart attack, as I told you, but gassed herself in the oven. She committed suicide.'

Time stood still; my head hurt as I tried to register what he was saying. I had an instant flashback. I could see Maude being carried away on a stretcher and the smell. What was the smell? Why couldn't I see Mum? Why couldn't I eat the food? Suicide. It must have been my fault. It couldn't have been Dad's fault so it must have been mine. I was hysterical. More pain. More lies exposed. It was unbearable. Blinded by tears, I stared, unable to speak. So many questions and now no voice. I ran up the stairs to my room. I cried, I howled. I curled up in a corner like a wounded animal and wondered how I could ever face tomorrow. Tears were something I had learned to hold back but now there was no stopping them; no matter how hard I tried to divert my attention, the tears kept flowing.

In the morning I woke. I knew something was different. For a split second I hoped it had all been a bad dream. Then I remembered. Maude. Suicide. The tears still flowed.

I went downstairs, dreading my breakfast with Dad. What could I say to him? Did we talk about it or not? Not a chance. We mumbled 'good morning' and avoided eye contact. Then Dad left hurriedly for work.

The opportunity to explore underneath, to look things in the face had gone. We had both avoided exploring Maude's death and bringing it to rest. I didn't realise then that by avoiding talking about Maude, we were both making a choice. We were saying, 'It's too much to change direction now.' Better the devil we know. Let sleeping dogs lie. But sooner or later, by making that choice, the dog turns into a monster: it comes up from the cellar and howls.

By the time I arrived at Wilkies, I was crying uncontrollably. The staff watched, embarrassed, and asked if there was anything they could do. I was silent. My eyes staring, lips tightly closed. The manager was called. No words came from me. He called a junior assistant to take me home. All I wanted to do was sleep, hoping that it would go away. I got into bed, pulled the covers around me and stared into space. When my father arrived home for lunch I felt so sorry for him that I couldn't cause him any more pain by asking him for an explanation, so I told him I had a sore stomach. I decided that if Dad could endure the pain, so could I, and I would forgive him. I blamed my mother for Dad keeping the truth from me.

That evening I decided to make him a meal and I emerged from my room with my head held high and a smile on my face as if nothing had happened. I began to cook, chatting to Dad about totally irrelevant subjects. This has been the story of my life – bury the truth and the pain and feel like an empty shell inside.

Much later in my life, I had a dream. I was revisiting our house in Kingsburgh Road. In the dream I was able to flit from room to room, as if I was in a spaceship, and view everything at high speed. I arrived at the house and immediately the whole front of it peeled away. I could see into the cellar, which was a warm, glowing, orange colour. I wanted to see more and immediately whisked upstairs. Here I went into a bedroom. It felt like wartime. Through a door I saw a nurse, and she was putting away starched white linen along narrow slatted shelves. This isn't my house, I thought. There's nothing here that I recognise. I went downstairs to the kitchen. It had been gutted out and modernised; it led out to the back garden which was down a level. I wanted to leave. On the way out it felt as if I was going over a huge ramp. I woke up.

Now I am beginning to understand what this dream was about. It was taking me back into my own house, the house of my soul, my birthright. But it was telling me what I would need to do to regain my soul. First, if you are going to reclaim your house, you have to go to the foundations. If your foundations are weak, the whole structure is weak. My cellar was a bright orange glow. In colour therapy this represents shock and trauma with a focus on eating disorders. As this is the most predominant colour in my dream, it shows that I still needed to face the trauma. Instead I whisk upstairs to the starched white. This is the bit which wants to remedy things so that they appear to be neatly put away and under control. This is what I was doing when I made a meal for Dad that evening, putting on my bright smile and keeping up the chatter, to keep the pain out. I wasn't actually *dealing* with the pain, I was determined to white it out. Then there was the kitchen, the place of nourishment. But in my dream it had been gutted out. And this is what happens if you hide things away, you yourself get gutted out. This is exactly what happened to me some years later. Last, but not least, is the ramp. What I really wanted to do was revisit my home, take a quick look and say 'Oh, yes, I understand, all is well' and dart off again to get on with whirling in space. But I crossed a ramp. A ramp slows you down. In many ways, it has taken the writing of this book for me to really start taking a look at my house again, a slow look, and to gently return to my own home.

Chapter Eleven

Now that I'm beginning to look at my own pain and the things I had tidied away, I can see other people's pain more clearly and what happens when they try to hide from it. With my own parents, it made Dad numb his pain with drink, and Mum fall seriously ill. At the time, I thought Mum had got her just desserts. I blamed her for having made Dad keep the truth from me about Maude's suicide but she was just a convenient peg for me to hang my own pain on. In my dream it was a nurse who was folding things away so tidily. I have recently begun to ask Mum more about her own life story. I've found out that she worked for the Red Cross. Actually she wanted to work for the Territorial Army because she thought it would be much more fun, but in the end, she chose to go and work for a bank, which seemed to offer her greater security.

I understand now why Mum tried to impose the same kind of limits on me as had been imposed on her. We tend to impose the same patterns and conditions of our own childhood onto our children. Like wheels within wheels, circles within circles, until the soul rebels and breaks the patterns that don't belong to it.

Despite being in hospital, Mum still managed to instruct me on my career. 'The Civil Service would be a good, stable job for you. You must make something of your life. Get a good career and you'll get a good pension.' I wasn't happy at Wilkies any longer. So I decided I might as well make the move she suggested. I applied to the Civil Service.

I got an interview and ended up working at a desk. The people around me were loud and gregarious but I was full of fear. I found it impossible even to open my mouth to say 'good morning'. I felt shut out, just as I'd felt as a young child, when I first went to school. My reaction was to revert to my old patterns of self-destructive behaviour. So what if they didn't like me? I would be rude and rebellious, I didn't give a shit. The only day I enjoyed was a Wednesday when I was supposed to go to college for day release study. However, if I had been out late the night before I spent the day in bed recovering.

One day at work I overheard a girl talking about her night job in a bar and how they were looking for staff. I pushed in and said, 'Me, I could do that.' They laughed, and for the next few weeks I sat with them quietly, not speaking. Slowly, however, they accepted that I was there and when one of them needed a night off at the bar, they asked me to cover for her.

I arrived at The Bandwagon, a pub with live music which was run by three brothers. I was very scared but before I knew it, I was given a tray, a pad and a pen and sent to work. This I really loved. People needed me and I didn't have to talk, just smile and take the orders. I didn't even have to add up the total as the person behind the bar did that. Tips of money and drink were given which we counted and divided up at the end of the evening; it was one of the most exciting parts of the job. Suddenly I found a new freedom. I became the extrovert with alcohol. People found me funny. They began to know me and call me by my name, and I drank more and more. When I was working at the pub at night and drinking a lot, my life seemed to be transformed and I was hooked.

My new-found freedom in the pub revolved around money, new clothes and hairstyles. I decided to dye my hair blonde and then I experimented with perms, all of which resulted in my hair becoming very dry and looking like straw. But still I persisted. I thought it was true that blondes had more fun and got more attention.

I was earning good money and moving in an adult world where nobody seemed to have any expectations of me. The Bandwagon introduced me to a whole new social life. I was socialising with a rich and powerful group of people, who to a large extent 'controlled' Edinburgh. They owned the night clubs and were forces to be reckoned with. I was only 16 or 17, gadding around in Rolls Royces and Mercedes. To a young, impressionable girl, the thought of going out with wealthy people twice your age, drinking all night with the top crowd, is highly attractive. I thought this was the right way to live and closed my eyes to the shady side of what went on. I enjoyed the excitement. It was an adrenalin kick. 'Nobody can touch me,' I thought, 'because I'm with the top people in Edinburgh.'

I met Shaun in The Bandwagon, an exceedingly handsome boy who I began to go out with. His temper and violence were things that in some strange way attracted me. I was not in love with him – I knew that – but he held a great fascination for me. It was something to do with never knowing where I was with him; it actually made me feel more alive, being on tenterhooks, wondering what would happen next. It didn't matter that he beat me up on several occasions, one time smashing a car window and pulling me through it. I revelled in the attention I received from this drama. Eventually he cheated on me and finished the relationship. I didn't like this at all, and later I made sure of my revenge.

I loved money and spent it all the time, buying an old heap of a car which was my pride and joy. I filled it with fluffy toys and had a large pair of brightly coloured dice hanging from the mirror. I had no driving licence or insurance and had only driven a couple of times before I careered around Edinburgh with total confidence – but totally illegally, of course. I drove my friend Tracy through to Glasgow. We stopped in the car park beside the railway station looking for a parking space when a policeman came over.

My heart began to beat very loud and fast, I wound down my window and, with an enormous show of confidence, asked him politely where I could park my car. I told him that we had just driven through from Edinburgh to see the sights and spend our money in the fabulous shops of Glasgow. The policeman said that I reminded him of his daughter and indicated a parking space. As the fear engulfed me I managed to find my voice. I smiled and thanked him and Tracy and I went off to spend some money and have lunch. When we returned to the car park, the car was still there with no police surrounding it. I couldn't believe my luck.

On our way home there was torrential rain. Water was pouring in and soaking my foot on the accelerator. It was going numb. I also realised we probably had a fuel leak. I cruised the car into the next garage on the dual carriageway and filled up with petrol, all the time wondering if the sales assistant would phone the police since I looked so young and the car was such a wreck. I proceeded to drive a short distance back down the dual carriageway, and crossed the central reservation to get to the traffic lights that would put me back on the road home to Edinburgh knowing, as I did, that we had a fuel crisis. By now Tracy was anything but amused and her nerves were shot to pieces. She wanted me to drop her off at the nearest railway station. I wouldn't hear of it. 'Just relax. Everything's fine,' I told her. I was loving it: music blaring, singing along and thinking to myself, this is the life.

I hid the fact that I had this car from my parents and parked it out of sight, up the road. They never knew, while most of Edinburgh, it seemed, did – having either pushed it, towed it or had a go at the mechanics. My friends began to refuse a lift even when I offered to run them home. Finally the car exploded and with sadness I had to get her towed away. The man who picked her up showed me part of the inside of the engine and explained that it was empty and should have had oil in it. He said he felt sorry for me and handed me the tax disc saying, 'At least you'll get a refund on this.'

In the meantime, Shaun had realised his mistake and was forever on the phone asking me out again. I played a waiting game. I told him I would go back out with him, but it was only so I could be the one to leave him in the lurch and pay him back for what he'd done to me.

My boss at the Civil Service checked the register for my day release at college and found that I had not attended in the last six months. I was given a stern warning. However, I was fed up having to explain every Wednesday off with lies that I was either at the dentist, the doctor or some other appointment and told them straight that I was leaving the Civil Service.

Many different jobs followed but I couldn't settle. I was always searching for something, still unsure of myself or what I was capable of doing, always acting on the outside as if nothing bothered me. I was constantly questioning who I was, what I was doing and where I was going. I had few social friends outside the pub and I couldn't stand being on my own. Deep down, I was very lonely.

Chapter Twelve

I was 17 years old, still young and flexible enough to chop and change direction. At that age it's easy to think it's just a question of spinning the wheel again and seeing if your lucky number comes up. My next spin of the wheel took me back to college full-time to do a course in business studies. My mother thought this would give me a better chance of earning a decent salary, but I didn't really enjoy it.

Unknown to me, the class entered me for the Edinburgh 'Charities' Queen' competition. At first I refused to go, but at the last minute I changed my mind and decided to go just for a laugh. The boys bought me a huge bouquet of red roses and we all gathered at my house so I could get ready. The contest was nerve wracking, but I managed to relax and have a good time.

Unbelievably to me, out of 60 contestants, I was one of the ones chosen for the top six, which meant we each had our photograph in the Edinburgh *Evening News* for a week. This gave everyone a chance to vote for the girl they thought should be the new Charities' Queen. I didn't win and was thankful since it would have been too much responsibility for me to have the position for a whole year. Nevertheless, because my photograph had been in the paper, people began saying to me that I looked like someone they knew, and it was this which prompted me to try to trace my natural mother.

I had fantasised often about her and now the realisation that I could actually meet her made me feel very excited. I went to Registry House where I was ushered into a room to be questioned about tracing my blood mother. They tried to put me off but I said it was absolutely pointless to try to dissuade me. I didn't need to be told the consequences. A short wait followed, and then the sudden reality of seeing my mother's name on a piece of paper, 'Anne Porteous'; a lovely name, I thought.

I had already worked out my plan of action and hurried along to the main post office where the telephone books for the whole of Scotland were kept. My birth certificate said that I had been born in Perth. Pulling out the relevant book, I could hardly turn the pages fast enough to get to P. My hands shook terribly. There, to my astonishment, was the name 'Porteous' under the same address as the one on my birth certificate. Without a moment's thought, I ran to the phone and dialled the number. A very amiable sounding lady answered and asked if she could help me. I blurted out who I was and suddenly there was a stony silence on the other end of the phone. Into the hollow mouthpiece I asked again if she knew who I was because my surname and the address on my birth certificate were the same as hers. I told her that I had been christened Jean Porteous, but still there was no reply. Then she said 'I do not know you, I cannot answer your questions,' and the phone went dead.

I held back the tears. I truly believed she would be delighted to hear from me. So why would she put the phone down? It didn't make sense. I wanted to believe she would want to hear from me again. I calmed down and decided to wait a few days before trying again. Armed this time with plenty of change, I called again and demanded to know what she knew about me. I told her I would keep calling until I got the truth. At first she denied everything, including that she had a daughter called Anne, but eventually she gave me the telephone number in Glasgow of a lady called Sarah, whom she claimed to be her only daughter. I rang the number immediately and the lady who answered told me her life story which seemed to have nothing whatsoever to do with me and she denied ever having heard about me. Despite her denial, I knew this number was a connection to my true mother; I even believed this woman might *be* my true mother. I felt defeated, angry and confused as it sank in that not even my 'real' mother wanted to speak to me, nor my 'real' grandmother. I gritted my teeth, my dreams smashed into bits. I hated the world.

This was a major upset and enough to justify my decision to drop out of college again. I went back to Wilkies, where I worked in the office, but after a few months I was made redundant. It came as a massive blow to me. It really upset me. I felt rejected. This added to my feelings of rejection by my blood mother and I cried incessantly. The truth was that Wilkies needed to make someone redundant and it made sense that it should be me since I was the last in, but that's not how I interpreted it.

The next spin of the wheel landed me a job with the British School of Motoring as a receptionist. I began checking people in for their lessons. All of the instructors were men and so was the boss. I used my new found feminine charms and was accepted by everyone who worked there.

By now my friends were beginning to leave The Bandwagon, new staff were filtering in and times were changing. I worked there less and less but I would still meet the boss and we would go out together, drinking in different pubs and clubs. I was enormously impressed with myself. The boss had an infamous reputation, and we were treated like honoured guests, always getting free drinks and food, everybody clustering round us, wanting to be in our company. This made me feel very powerful. I was even more impressed with myself because I refused to have a sexual relationship with him, despite his advances.

Then one day the news broke that the boss had been arrested for fraud at his betting shops and was awaiting trial. Slowly the regular customers began to leave The Bandwagon. When the boss was in jail, certain people came and smashed up the pub and fights became a regular occurrence. Sometimes while I was working behind the bar, bottles and glasses hurtled towards us as the fighting broke out. Several times people were sent flying through windows. As the violence took over, the regulars left. I handed in my notice too: all the fun had gone. I felt as if my second 'family' had been taken away from me. I had been there for one and a half years. Now there was nothing left and the excitement was gone. I felt gutted. Sadly, I moved on.

Chapter Thirteen

At BSM, my boss began to get on at me for not eating enough. At first I didn't believe him but he told me repeatedly that I wasn't eating. I felt I didn't need food. I was well. I had energy. I was fine. I didn't feel the need to recollect what or when I last ate. It wasn't important and part of me believed that I was eating. If I wanted to eat, then I would. My boss nagged and nagged and wouldn't give up. He kept telling me I was getting thinner. I didn't think so. In fact, I thought I looked good. My clothes looked good, my figure looked good, I had so much energy and I was alive.

People looked at me. Men looked at me. When people looked, they were admiring me and I knew that because I *did* look good. Eventually, my boss demanded that I eat something in front of him to prove I was eating. How dare he treat me like this? If I wanted to eat I would. What was it to do with him? My anger overwhelmed me. I felt like a child and wanted to cry. I felt this man was looking into my soul. He was looking into something that was very private. This was my life, not anybody else's, and I knew my own needs. With anger, tears and frustration bottling up inside me I determined to prove him wrong, so I stormed off to the local Chinese restaurant and ordered some food. When it arrived, I physically wasn't able to put it into my mouth. I sat and I stared at it. I couldn't eat it. I wondered then how long it was since I had eaten anything. I couldn't remember. The meal in front of me felt as if it was already in my stomach, churning around and around. A feeling of sickness welled up inside me as if it was coming into my mouth and I would actually be sick, yet the food in front of me was my favourite food, chicken and sweetcorn with fried rice. I was frightened. The more I wanted to eat, the more I began to panic. There was no way that this food could possibly go into my mouth. My arm felt as though it weighed a ton, I couldn't even lift the fork to put food on it. I stared at the untouched plate in front of me. My eyes felt glazed. I was confused and worried, then suddenly the words of my boss echoed over and over in my head. I realised that I had a serious problem.

In my mind I began to look back at my life and mealtimes with my parents. If I chose to sit quietly, I got into trouble for being silent. On the other hand, if I spoke I got into trouble, too, for saying the wrong thing. I often refused food, especially sweets or desserts. My mother always made a scene about what she called 'your so-called diet'. The more she went on, the less I wanted to eat anything. When I looked at the table and us sitting there in our falseness, I realised I had chosen not to eat with my parents. So if I wasn't eating with them, when did I eat?

I knew I had eaten lunch when I first started with BSM, but when did I stop? I couldn't answer the question. My boss had obviously noticed that I had stopped eating so maybe he would know, and yet I wasn't able to ask him. I was too frightened. I hadn't eaten breakfast for a long time either. Usually, Dad made breakfast for everyone and it was always a 'fry up', but I couldn't remember the last time I had eaten it. I would fall out of bed and go to work, lucky to be on time. Gradually, I began to realise that I hadn't eaten for a long time, so what would I do? What could I do? My alcohol levels I knew were very high. At night we would go to a club where a bottle of Vodka or Bacardi would easily be put down. By now I was also smoking 20 cigarettes a day. I began to realise my life was a blur.

I realised that I wasn't clear about a lot of things. Everything just consisted of me laughing, having fun, living life in the fast lane. But what lay behind all the speed? What did I talk about, what was I doing, where had I been? I really could no longer tell. I was seeing life through a haze of alcohol. It was obvious I needed to cut down and get some food inside me. I knew very drastic measures were needed. It was extremely difficult, but I managed by making myself take just a teaspoon of food at a time. I put it on a saucer, and forced myself to eat it. Bit by bit, I increased the amount over the following weeks and months. I simply had to get back into a routine of putting food into my mouth and chewing it. Gradually I began to accept food again.

Chapter Fourteen

While my mother had been in hospital, I had had the run of the house and Dad was happy to let me do as I pleased. After seven months and a successful heart operation, Mum returned home. She was back to take over again and I resented it. We fell back into a power struggle, fighting for control in the house, vying with each other for my father's attention. To an outsider, the solution was obvious, we needed to be separated. I needed a place of my own, but it took a crisis to bring this about.

I was trying to establish my personality and I did that by battling against hers. One minute our relationship was very good and the next it was very bad. She was nearly 40 when she married my father, and 'inherited' a child that wasn't hers; she had to give up a good job in the bank to look after me. I was a very jealous child and she told me she couldn't have children because I was too jealous. I did care for her. I needed a mother and there were times she really was a mother to me. Then I would feel an immense wave of love for her, but almost as soon as it came it would be followed by a wave of hate. Love in hate, and hate in love. I was truly confused.

I felt I wasn't allowed my own life. I wasn't allowed just to be myself. I didn't know how to escape from being who my parents wanted me to be. I felt different from the rest of the family. Academically they all did well, almost all of them going to University while I circled around with no foundation, no steady job and no marriage on the horizon.

One day things came to a head. I was running into the house in my usual hurry, and I was desperate for the toilet. I met my mother, who stood in front of me, arms outstretched, barring my way. My blood boiled and my anger became too explosive to contain. I warned her to move out of my way. She stood her ground. I warned her again; she was as determined as I was. I gave her one more warning and then I did it. I shoved past her and she fell, snagging her leg on a piece of wire sticking out of a grocery box. It started to bleed; even in my fury I knew that this time I had gone too far. It was risky for her to get a cut or even a scratch. She was on Warfarin after her heart operation because her blood didn't clot properly. Now I had inflicted bodily harm and with the thought of this stigma forever on my head and everybody in the family thinking I was dangerous and aggressive, I decided I had to leave. Rumours would spread that I had tried to murder Mum. I was so sure of this that I didn't even try to tell my own version of things, that Mum was always trying to bar me in one way or another, and this time it had been once too much. All I had done was try to get to the toilet. I packed my bags and left home, vowing never to return. I found a flat to rent and moved in with my friend Maxi.

Within eight months I was home again. It's interesting now being able to look back and question what kept me tied to my parents' house when inside I was screaming to get away, to be independent. I think it was a fear of the unknown, the black hole of uncertainty that lay outside. Better the devil I knew. But I was caught in a trap and became more and more unstable.

My first attempt to live independently ended up with the fire-brigade! One night I came back pretty drunk, went to bed and lit a cigarette. I must have nodded off because the next thing I knew, the bed was on fire. I put my coat and slippers on and ran into Maxi's room to tell her I had set my bed on fire and then carried on running, out of the flat, onto the pavement, and hailed a taxi. I didn't give a shit. I was hungry and knew a place that stayed open until 4.00 a.m.

At the Metropole Restaurant, still only wearing my tweed coat and black fluffy slippers, I devoured a double hamburger and chips, then hailed another taxi to take me back to the flat. I arrived to find an outraged Maxi. The fire-brigade had been, my bed was a charred mess and the whole flat was reeking of smoke. I just plonked myself down on the sofa and fell asleep. We didn't have much choice after that but to leave. Maxi moved in with her boyfriend, and I, having nowhere else to go, moved back home.

Not long after that my parents decided to sell the house and it felt as if my foundations were collapsing once again. I felt this house held some kind of basis for my existence. I couldn't imagine life without Kingsburgh Road. Kingsburgh Road was my home. It was unthinkable to me that they could sell it. Dad said it was due to my mother's heart condition, she could no longer climb the stairs. It was a bitter blow having to pack everything up and move. It triggered a fear in me, yet I didn't know why. I begged them not to sell it. We wouldn't be able to take everything with us to the new house and so things that had belonged to me, my bedroom furniture, would be gone, never to be seen again.

Soon after we moved Shuna had to be put down and I lost my faithful friend who had been with me all through my early years. I didn't cry. I told myself she would be better off, yet inside I was really crying and found it hard to accept she was not going to be around any more. I tried to push down the pain by going out that night and drinking myself into a sodden blur.

My parents had already planned their holiday to St Andrews and because I wasn't allowed to stay in the new house on my own, I had to go with them. Luckily, for the first time, I was allowed to take a friend with me. I chose Donna. Aged 18, we were wild teenagers together, going out at night, drinking and smoking, and having a good time. I didn't care about the consequences. In the event, I got such bad cystitis I had to go into hospital for a D and C. But still I continued to drink. I loved St Andrews; we made new friends and I fell in love with a boy called Dougie and wished I could stay there with him.

A few days back in Edinburgh and my mother and I were screaming blue murder at each other. I realised I couldn't continue to stay at home and so I picked up the phone and called my new-found friends in St Andrews. I asked them if they could find me a job. Within a few days, Donna and I returned to St Andrews to become chambermaids at the Old Course Hotel. Our new lives had begun.

Chapter Fifteen

Freedom at last! I was quite settled working at the Old Course Hotel. Many other young people worked there too, so every night became a social gathering in the local pub. We drank, smoked and had fun. Our wages never seemed to be enough and we were always running out of money, but I felt happy and loved the sea and the beautiful sunrises and sunsets. The relationship between Dougie and me continued and although his interest seemed to be lagging, I persisted, I needed him, and I lived in fear of rejection.

Donna and I had been at the Old Course Hotel throughout the summer and now the season was ending. We accepted a transfer to London and had a farewell party in the pub. I thought Dougie would beg me to stay but instead he ignored me. For all these months Dougie had been oblivious to Donna's advances but now she seized her moment and flirted with him all night, never letting him out of her sight. My tolerance was burnt out. I grabbed her by the throat and shook her. I had no idea what I was doing. Donna and I went back to the hotel in silence. I was seething with rage and fell into a troubled sleep. In the morning Donna refused to come to London with me but I knew there was nothing for me in Edinburgh. I couldn't go back to stay with my parents and so I made my decision to go to London alone.

On arriving at the railway station, I saw Donna and my heart soared. We forgot our fight, forgave each other and set off on a new adventure.

When we arrived in London my first impression was that it was so enormous it would be easy to feel abandoned and lost, but I didn't get lost, I loved it. I had finally made the break from my parents and for the first time in my life I realised that I was a natural loner – whereas up to that point it had been horrendous for me to be alone, I had to go out every night, have lots of friends, socialise. Suddenly in London that all changed: I found I enjoyed being alone. If I did want company there was Donna and other people in the hotel that I liked and got on with. It was good living and working in the same place. You had people there if you wished, but you could also be on your own. I enjoyed living like that.

There was a funny incident when we first arrived in London. Our room was on the top floor of the hotel and Donna had put her shoes and a haggis which she'd brought with her from Edinburgh on the window ledge. Her shoes fell off the ledge and so did the haggis and she had to explain to the housekeeper why she needed the keys for the basement below our window. We told everyone the story that haggis can fly and how it had flown out of the window trying to make its way back home. Because the window ledge was so high up, not like in the Scottish Highlands where they just run around the heather, it had fallen. We had a really good laugh about that.

In the hotel they were very mean with the food and didn't allow us chambermaids, the lowest ranking in the hotel, to have salad. The more senior staff sat at a different side of the dining hall where all the tasty salads and other forbidden foods were laid out. We were always starving and only got paid £18 a week, which we used to spend in a local pub called the Villiers. We would go there on a Thursday and stockpile ourselves with food, eating as many as three meals, one after the other.

One day at the hotel, however, they served us what they called Irish stew, which amounted to some water with about four bones swimming on a plate. I flipped and took the plate with the gravy swishing all over the place straight to the manager's office, and I flung it on his desk. The gravy went everywhere and I said to him, 'You eat it.' He was raging, telling me I would get sacked. I said, 'No, we want salad. I'm not leaving this office – I'm on a sit-down strike until you tell me that you will respect us like human beings. We may have a 'lower-class' job, but we're no different from anybody else.' He kept threatening to sack me but I persisted, 'You can't.' I knew he had gone out with Donna one night and given her drugs, because she came back that night and tried to fly out the window. She genuinely thought she could fly. I had to hold her back because she was off her face. I said to him, 'If you want to sack me and go down that road, I'll report you – I have witnesses to what happened that night.' So I stubbornly sat there until he said, 'Okay, you can have salad.' I left his office and said, 'Guess what? We can have salad. Let's go,' and we all charged into the dining-room and tore into the food. It was fun but my days were numbered, obviously, because I was starting to become a nuisance and a trouble maker.

As ever, things change, but this time I instigated the change. I wasn't enjoying the work any more and I didn't like the hotel. It was right beside Charing Cross station and didn't let in much light, which I found depressing. There were no sunsets or sunrises, or the smell of the sea like in St Andrews. Instead there was the smog, the fumes of city life and the greyness of the hotel. This was also around the time that the IRA bombs were going off in London and you could almost believe you were in World War Two, sheltering in the hotel basement until it was safe to come out.

When I left I had nowhere to go and moved in with a guy called Richard that I'd been seeing for a while. He lived in the wildest of flats – all red; every wall, every floor, every ceiling, every room was red. Red everywhere. What I didn't know was that he and his friends were all on drugs. I refused to swallow pills, I wouldn't inject; in fact, I'd only ever smoked dope, but they were into cocaine and all sorts. I didn't understand at first why the people were so weird and wore dark glasses indoors. If I'd been really observant I would have noticed, or perhaps I was just naïve. Then one night I did snort something which made me sneeze and they were raging that I'd sneezed this good stuff out. However, some of it had stayed up my nose and sent me off my rocker. At one point I actually felt very good, as if I could jump off a skyscraper. I vowed I'd never do it again, though, because the 'down' was too horrible. I had no money and wasn't working. I was literally stealing milk off people's doorsteps.

By now Donna was spending a lot more time with her boyfriend. They'd go away at weekends and our friendship was beginning to drift apart as we went our own ways. I went back to the Villiers to ask for a job because I knew the people there. They gave me a new job and a place to stay.

From then on I went out with the DJ, Steve, and that was fine for a while. He came from Cornwall and we went to Cornwall a couple of times but it was the image I wanted, not the person. All the girls fancied him because he was a DJ. While I was behind the bar at the Villiers I would watch Steve running the disco and eventually I decided I could be a DJ myself. I went to a club one night without him, approached the manager and said, 'I'm a DJ and I'm looking for work – I'm excellent, I'm the best.' I really built myself up but in truth, I didn't even know how to play a record. I mimicked everything I'd learnt from my viewpoint behind the bar, and the guy gave me a job saying I could start the following night. I didn't turn up, of course.

I knew that Steve and I weren't working out. I knew I had to move on, to be on my own, and I began to look around for another job. I saw one advertised which said 'Mascot Telephone Answering, and accommodation'. This appealed to me since I also needed somewhere to stay. I had no idea what telephone answering was but I called the woman and with an air of confidence I told her that I was the one for the job. Then I phoned her back and said, 'Look, I have other job offers, have you made your decision yet? I can't hang around,' and she said 'Yes.' So I got the job and moved in. She left me on my own on the first day – it was mayhem but I began to slot in. I could see how the system worked. I talked to people, I was in charge of staff and I had a great time. We answered for all sorts of well-known people – musicians, writers, businessmen. This was a happy time, I loved it.

I came into my own. I felt part of something. We organised promotions for Capital Radio: we put out questions, for instance, to which we would give prizes for the best-quip answer. I warned BT that we hadn't enough 'safe lines'. Safe lines are when you have banks of phones, and from outside you can dial one of several numbers, each with one digit changed, eg. 2222, 2223 and 2224. If the numbers aren't in consecutive order, they aren't safe. I warned BT that the numbers wouldn't hold. 'It's Capital Radio,' I said, 'and we're going to get bombed out with this.' We put out a question, 'Why Martini Bianco?' and it was my job to pick the wittiest answer. In the first hour we blew up the whole exchange, the calls were going everywhere and I thought it was brilliant. These competitions were fun, fast, exciting.

London gave me a sense of real freedom because it was such an enormous place and I was able to jump on a tube and go anywhere I wanted. Instead of hanging my head and thinking 'woe is me', there was a character emerging. I did a lot more than any of my friends. At Mascot I was more or less running the business because the boss was an alcoholic and rarely turned up. I'd progressed from being a 'silly wee lassie', running around Scotland like a headless chicken wondering who I was going to go out with next, to suddenly being in a position of responsibility. I realised then that if you have someone telling you what to do you don't think for yourself, but when there's nobody, you just have to get on with it, you have no choice. The responsibility gave me confidence and I began to change. I began to grow up. I loved my job and I didn't want to lose it. I had a good relationship with all the customers, feeling as I did that I was playing a key role in their success. They'd rely on me and phone in saying 'Hi, Alison, have you got any messages for me?'. It made me see life in a different way. For the first time I had to learn to have boundaries – especially with the staff, being their friend one day and then sometimes having to sack them the next. It was very difficult but a huge element of maturity came into it. Until then, I had been trying to find my idea of freedom in booze, cigarettes and dope, which gave me a false kind of high. Now I had to get my life together, so I stopped drinking almost entirely and just smoked marijuana.

I would roll two joints, cook my tea, eat, and then smoke all night, sitting in a chair on my own with my music, usually Leonard Cohen. His lyrics reflected my soul's quest and I would sing along with him, asking questions, Who am I? Where am I going? Why am I here? A lot of people say his music is depressing, but I don't agree: I think his lyrics helped me to search deeper into myself, and 'Sisters Of Mercy' was one of my favourites. The only problem was I was usually too stoned to concentrate and I was amused at the fact that I was too out of it to find the answers, although I enjoyed the meditative state. I was dependent on the dope to bring me into a state of deeper awareness, so it hardly gave me answers, but it was a start.

I did this for nearly a year, sitting in on my own at night smoking dope, asking questions, seeking answers. Something I did recognise was that nobody knew me – I could build a character and so I began to create the voice, the speech, the look, the style, the personality of a new me. At the same time, I enjoyed going out. London was like a merry-go-round of intense work and equally intense fun, and a new discovery of myself.

Chapter Sixteen

I was in London for a total of seven years and occasionally went back to Edinburgh to see friends, always going home for Christmas. For a while I had a boyfriend in Edinburgh called Alan. He was a social worker and I visited him regularly.

One of my visits to Edinburgh centred around my old school friend Gillian's wedding. We had been friends since we were little and looked so alike that teachers used to get us mixed up. This we took full advantage of, sometimes swapping hockey matches with each other just for the fun of seeing if anyone would notice. Gillian had gone out with her boyfriend since the age of 14, and at 21 they decided to get married. She invited me to the wedding. I didn't have much money but I managed to get her a present and myself a train ticket to Edinburgh. It was wonderful to see her and all of my old friends again. Just six months later I got a phone call in London. It was to tell me that Gillian had died. She had been ill and ended up in a wheelchair and then in hospital. I was devastated. No one had told me. Neither Tracy nor Moira had called to let me know what was happening.

Her death affected me profoundly. I couldn't understand why she had to die. She had everything to live for. Me, I had nothing, I had no one. So why was it not me? Gillian had it all to look forward to. She had found her happiness. She never drank or smoked, so why her? I searched my soul for answers, asking the same old questions, What was life about? Why was I here? Why did I feel this deep loneliness? Waves of depression swept over me and I felt the emptiness inside me again. I had many dreams in which she was alive. In one of the dreams she asked me to accept her death. I eventually did come to terms with it and the dreams stopped.

I was lost and lonely until one day, life became worth living again. I met the man of my dreams. Immediately, I thought, 'This is it, this is what life is about!' And I fell madly in love. Within four months we had a house together.

John was a driving instructor, handsome, slightly older than me and incredibly wonderful in my eyes. I always knew I would fall in love instantly and this was 'it'.

John fitted into my attraction list. He was a very masculine figure, in control and self-assured. He was also a challenge because at first he didn't pay much attention to me although I was determined that he would. Yet it was more than that – because the moment I saw him I thought this man was the man of my dreams. Whether or not it was some kind of karmic link between us, it was certainly an incredibly powerful attraction. He was also a womaniser, I knew that, but I decided I would be the woman who would change his life. I would prove how worthy I was, how beautiful and how wonderful I was, if I could tame this man into being with me. For a while I did.

I thought John and I would get married; it was what I wanted. We settled into a house in Milton Keynes. It was a council house but it was beautiful to me. I thought at that point that this was it: I was in love with this man, I had my house and I was going to settle down.

I felt safe with John and told him everything. I told him the story of my adoption and, of course, he asked if I'd met my birth mother. This brought it all back to the surface again. At the same time, I had a premonition that Dad was going to die. I could feel it, I could see it, just as I could see when someone was ill when I was younger. I just knew he was going to die. I still considered him my dad even though I had experienced the shocking revelation that he wasn't; he was still the only one and I knew he loved me. My dad's love never wavered for me so I'm sure it was this fear of him dying that prompted me finally into making the decision, while my dad was alive, to find my blood mother. I wanted to be honest with him about trying to trace her and felt intuitively that I had to do it while he was still alive.

It wasn't just a one-way thing, it was something he had to do too.

Yet, for all my intuition about Dad, I put off tracing my natural mother. Life with John was my immediate concern, and it wasn't going smoothly. I was trying my best to be the proper little housewife, but found that despite my early training, I was always getting into domestic dramas. I remember one time we'd just had a beautiful white carpet laid, and I put on the washing machine and nipped out for a packet of cigarettes. When I came back, the machine had flooded all over the new carpet. I was horrified, but John used the occasion to lash out at me. He could see I didn't fit the domestic bill, yet he also, perversely, wanted to keep me a prisoner in our home.

A year later Sheriff Officers arrived at our house. John had told me he had been married and had a young child, but his wife had left him for another man. The truth was that he had been married twice before and he had five children, not one, and now the officers were here to bring him to court for not paying maintenance. When I saw the child at the court hearing he tried to deny it was his but I worked out that the night I met him, his wife must have been six or seven months' pregnant. His relationship with her was over by that time, but now I knew I could never trust him again. I couldn't believe he would deny his own son and lie like this.

My heart was breaking. I knew I should leave him. He began to womanise and the more he womanised, the more he believed that I was looking at other men and the more jealous he became. He became increasingly angry, paranoid and suspicious. At parties I had to stand on my own while he chatted to other women. If any man dared to talk to me, there was hell to pay.

I found myself one night looking up at the stars, something I couldn't remember doing since I was a child. I asked for help and guidance on how to get out of the mess I was in. I knew now I had to go home. I knew my dad was going to die soon. I knew I had to find my natural mother. There was so much about my life that I didn't know and now I needed to find some answers.

Edinburgh was calling. The only way I could see of getting back to Scotland was to go with John, so I planted the seed in his mind that this move could be our new start. He could set up his own driving school there and everything would be all right. He agreed, although he wouldn't let me take my lovely dog. John hated the dog so I gave him away, feeling that this would give him a better life. I missed that dog and it hurt. We exchanged our house in Milton Keynes with some people who lived in Musselburgh, close to Edinburgh, and I came home.

Not long after returning to Edinburgh, my mother telephoned to say that Dad was going into hospital for tests on his heart.

Chapter Seventeen

I took out my birth certificate and phoned the number in Perth. This time when I called I pretended to be a friend of Anne's and the woman replied that her daughter Anne was living locally and gave me the number. I called Anne and told her who I was. I said I wanted to meet her. I called my father and told him that I had contacted my natural mother. He was pleased and said, 'Alison, you need to do this. I'll help you, but I don't want to meet her. It's something you need to do for yourself.' The arrangements made, Dad offered to drive me to Perth for the meeting.

I was 24. Dad remained unwell and was going through more tests. My big day of meeting my mother had arrived and Dad drove me to Perth, kissed me and wished me well. Brenda came too and just shrugged and smiled, telling me not to expect too much. I didn't. Or did I?

Anne's husband met me first and instantly expressed his amazement at my resemblance to her and her family. He told me she was nervous, but she knew she had to see me and all would be well. My first impression of her was how alike we were; her mannerisms and looks and attitude. She had a council house in the way I had always imagined. I felt instantly at home.

I warmed to my half-brother, Keith, immediately. We shared many interests: bikes, cars, foods, habits and a sense of fun. My half-sister, Clare, smiled at me and made me feel welcome. I began to relax and feel 'myself' and I wondered why. I began to see similarities between us all and these similarities were not bad. These were good people. They were kind and caring, and I began to see a part of me that I had never seen before. I stayed the whole weekend, the first of many. By the end of it, my real mum had filled me in with many details.

Anne told me that my father had raped her; he didn't have a job and he drank. She was 15 when she got pregnant and, admittedly very naïve, only found out she was pregnant when she went into hospital for an operation on her appendix. Despite the circumstances, she chose to continue with the pregnancy, but her mother was a snob and sent her away from Perth to Edinburgh to work until I was born.

As my mother showed me around her house I noticed an old photograph of a woman who was strikingly similar to myself. On asking who it was, I discovered it was my grandmother, her mother. I showed my mother the telephone number that I called originally and asked whose it was. She replied that it was my grandmother's. I then told her the story of the first time I tried to find her when I was 16 and how I had been given the phone number of someone in Glasgow. When I finished telling her my mother's eyes opened wide and in a quiet voice she asked me to confirm that I had tried to find her when I was 16. I nodded and she erupted into a rage, upset that she hadn't been told about my efforts to contact her.

I found out that Anne's sister, Sarah, was the woman I had spoken to in Glasgow, a neurotic who had taken early retirement because she was emotionally unstable. She fell in love when she was just 18 but her parents forced her to go to university instead of being with her true love and apparently she never recovered.

Anne went on to tell me that I was born in one of those unmarried mother's homes and she had been forced by her parents to put me up for adoption. According to her, the separation broke her heart. I loved this story; it made me feel wanted. She told me she had always looked for me and kept a photo of me which she carried next to her heart. I had always known she loved me and was looking for me. At last I felt I could begin to work out my life.

A year later, the devastating news that she had applied to emigrate to Canada made me feel as if my whole world was collapsing yet again. I was fated not to have a mother. How could life deal me such a cruel blow? I was really confused.

During the remaining time we had together I slowly began to see another side to her. My fairy tale image of this woman was fading as I began to wake up to her as a real person and not a fantasy. She was unpredictable and selfish and her attitude from time to time seemed strange. It made me feel there was more to our story than I had been told. Underneath the caring, I saw a hard streak. I began to distrust her. I wanted to know more – there were things that didn't make sense to me and I wanted to know about my real father in particular. I knew there were still pieces of the jigsaw missing. We remained friends however, and after a sad parting my new family was gone.

At home, my relationship with John was becoming very difficult. The driving school business was going well but it gave John ample opportunity to womanise. He had hit me several times and I knew it was time to leave. The difficulty was that we had borrowed money to invest in the business and I had no means of escape. He didn't allow me to work or go out with my friends, at times even locking me in the house. One night I did go out and left him a salad for when he came home from work. When I arrived back, he had ripped the cooker out of the wall. If he was not going to get hot food, then neither would I. The second time I went out with my friend I was locked out and he wouldn't let me in, so the next day I took my clothes and left everything else. I took no calls from him, nor did I phone him. All my furniture, the things I had worked for, all the carpets, the whole house, I left everything. I had nothing except the clothes I was standing in.

I had nowhere to go, no job, no money. My only escape now was to go back to my parents' house with my tail between my legs. My mother had never liked John, she could see he wasn't a particularly good person: 'He's a cheat, a liar and he'll have other affairs.' To be fair, her intuition was right.

Chapter Eighteen

I got a new job telephone answering for a company called Aircall. One night I had been working late, and a friend and I decided to go to the pub for a drink. When we got there I saw a man looking at me with interest from the other end of the bar. He came over and offered me a drink which I accepted, and we began to talk. Then a fight broke out; glass was flying everywhere and he shielded me with his jacket. I thought, 'How sweet, he's trying to protect me. Here's someone who cares enough.' Because of the fight we moved to another pub and talked until seven in the morning. I really liked him and found him interesting and easy to talk to. He was a lovely man and when he asked me out, that was it. I became excited about our meetings.

There is no question in my mind that Ramon and I were meant to meet that night. We had already met when I was five, because his aunt lived next door to us. Our paths were linked. I believe that God works with precision planning. We can try to control our lives as much as we like, but there's also another force at work, shaping our destiny. How many times have you heard of people being in the wrong place at the wrong time, or others narrowly avoiding death because obstacles were put in their way? You hear people saying 'There must have been an angel watching over them, it wasn't their time.' I don't believe anything happens by chance – neither the big things like being born or dying, nor the small things like finding the teapot you have always wanted in a junk shop. My belief is that God works in mysterious ways and we cannot see the bigger picture. Life holds its own rhythm of change, and we need to tune into that rhythm, not try to go against it, or refuse to adapt to the natural cycle of growing and ageing. Once you get in tune, doors open up as if by magic. I believe that when I met Ramon we were both in tune. This doesn't mean we saw the bigger picture, as God sees it. I'm not sure if that is possible, but we can all ask God for guidance, to help us step out of our little picture into His bigger picture, into His Divine plan.

I knew my parents would like Ramon and for the first time it seemed as if I was doing everything right. I was a bit concerned about taking him home, yet at the same time I knew he was very acceptable and that Mum would be falling all over him.

I was right. As soon as I brought him home, Mum pronounced, 'He's a good man!' But the sweetness of hearing her say that was immediately soured when she let slip the comment, 'Of course, Alison has gone out with a lot of other men.' I was raging, justifiably so. I wish I'd found the strength to say to her, 'Look – that really hurt me, why did you say that?' It would have cleared the air. But I didn't have the insight then; I was far too eaten up with the drama of it all to have insights. Nevertheless for the time being, Ramon's love kept me buoyant.

With Ramon I felt safe and secure; I felt loved. We would wine and dine and go out to parties and although I was drinking in moderation, it was still more than the majority of people. I was thin, I didn't eat a lot, but I did feel good and now I had Ramon, who could show me a different side of Edinburgh life. I now had a man to drive me around, to escort me to different places and have fun with. I no longer had to wonder what the prices in restaurants were or if I'd have to pay my way – there was none of that, he was the gentleman. He had a yellow Mercedes, and owned a snooker club. I was amazed when he first took me to the club because all the famous snooker players were there.

Ramon's lineage was Italian, and he was expected to marry Italian blood. His parents, wondering where he was, night after night, worried that he might be gambling and eventually put a tail on him. They found out he was dating me. I was then invited to meet his family and I vividly remember the table being covered with wonderful food: it was literally groaning under the weight of vast quantities of pork, steak, lamb chops, side dishes of salads, cooked vegetables, pasta and potatoes. It looked wonderful, but due to my nerves, I could hardly eat a thing. During the meal, Ramon spoke to his mother in Italian, gesticulating wildly to express what he wanted. This was a natural Italian way of life. I perceived this as rude and belittling, but they found it natural; it was a language they were all used to. All I could think was, 'There's no chance I'd jump if Ramon did that to me!'

His mother and father had an ice cream shop in Edinburgh and Ramon had worked in it when he was young. He was a businessman from a very early age and the family worked its way up in life through hard work, owning cafés, bookies, taxis and always ploughing their money back in. They had a lovely house in Lanark Road and Ramon still lived there. He had his own room, came and went as he pleased, he was fed, had all his washing done, and his mother jumped if he snapped his fingers. She was a lovely and very beautiful woman. His father's attentions were directed into the business, which was very much the male role.

I'm glad I met Ramon before my dad died. Soon after we met, Dad had his heart operation, which was successful, but still, somewhere along the line, I couldn't believe what the doctors were saying. He certainly looked well and began to take up his walking again, yet still I heard this voice telling me he wouldn't be with us for much longer.

Ramon and Dad had things in common. I identified with Ramon's gentleness and his ability to answer my questions. My father had an incredible memory for facts and Ramon was exactly the same in that respect. It was just bliss to listen to them. And that was another thing that attracted me to Ramon, his intelligence. I could always ask my dad 'why?' and he always had an answer, even if it meant him looking it up. I could do exactly the same with Ramon, so I was now living my life with him as I had done with my father. Ramon wore a tweed jacket, my dad wore a tweed jacket. Although there were also differences, in essence they were the same, very soft, gentle, caring, loving. I knew my father was going to die and now I had found someone to replace him.

Part Three

Marriage and Breakdown

Chapter Nineteen

On the doctor's insistence, I had a pregnancy test. I had been feeling increasingly tired, and simply put it down to the recovery stages of glandular fever. Nevertheless, the doctor thought I should have the test as a 'routine' measure, to eliminate pregnancy as a possible cause of my tiredness. I was on the pill and had been told by the hospital two years earlier that I would not be able to have children due to severe scarring left by endometriosis. They told me that if I didn't get pregnant within six months, I never would.

When I phoned for the results and they said 'positive', I replaced the receiver and felt numb. The first thing I did was hoover the flat. I scrubbed and cleaned it from top to bottom, something I wasn't usually prone to doing. I couldn't believe this was happening to me.

I was frightened, more than I had ever been before. I knew that I had to tell Ramon. I also knew that I would have to tell my mother and suffer her reaction. Everything swirled around in my head. How was I going to tell Ramon? We went out for a meal and I held it in throughout until I remember having a pancake and ice cream and somehow the words just came out. I was absolutely hysterical. Ramon was as surprised as I was and worried at how he would break it to his family. On the other hand, it confirmed a prediction he'd been given three years earlier.

This is Ramon's story:

One Saturday in June 1979, my then girlfriend, Joyce, rang me and asked if I would drive her over to Balloch on the west coast of Scotland. She had booked us both an appointment with a clairvoyant. At the time, I was amused. I was a staunch Roman Catholic and had no interest in occultism. We travelled over to Balloch that day and arrived around lunchtime. Joyce suggested I go first.

On entering the room, the clairvoyant told me I was going on a cruise soon. I was amazed. I had booked to go on a cruise that following Monday. I didn't tell her this, but I was thinking, 'clever lady, lucky guess'. She said she was glad I had come because a spirit had entered the room and was now communicating with her. She continued with several predictions, including one that my great aunt would die of bowel cancer. (She did in fact die within six months of this disease). The clairvoyant said that in three years' time I would marry 'a nurse that's not a nurse, a blonde that's not a blonde' and that we would have two children, a boy and then a girl.

Although a sceptic, I took note of what she said and thought, 'We'll see!' However I felt a very strong force in the room when the spirit entered to deliver this knowledge. Before I left, the clairvoyant told me she had been communicating with my grandfather. She described him just as I remembered him. This proves to me there is life after death. My view now is that when we die we are reunited with our loved ones and then we are reborn.

Three years later, true to the prediction, I met Alison.

At the time Ramon and I met I was working for Aircall, telephone answering for the doctor's service. I was also still dying my hair blonde. Another interesting thing is that Ramon and I went on holiday to Balloch, where he'd been given the prediction, and that's where our son Daryl was conceived. On reflection, I believe that a soul enters at the point of conception and there's no question in my mind now that this was the case. Daryl's soul was coming in to Ramon and me and he came in at exactly that point in time. It was written in the stars. It had been predicted.

Although confused, I was adamant that I wouldn't have an abortion. I knew that if my mother had aborted me I wouldn't be alive now. It wasn't in my nature to harm anything, I couldn't kill anything that had a life form. I was going to have this baby whether he stuck by me or not. We decided to get married. I had to stop drinking and smoking because I was throwing up everywhere. My life began to change. I thought it would all be better when the baby was born and I'd get my figure back and start smoking and drinking again.

We announced our forthcoming marriage. Everyone was delighted and our parents met each other and were pleased. I felt as if my life was running away with me, out of my control. I couldn't even drink or smoke to blot it out. Suddenly the wedding was no longer a good idea but a concrete reality. Everyone else was busy organising my life. The wedding day got closer and life became a whirlwind of arrangements and invitations.

I wanted to fulfil my pact with Moira – I wanted her to be my bridesmaid. My mother stepped in and said it was impossible, she was abroad and we wouldn't be able to get her fitted for a dress in time. I was adamant, but my mother insisted on having her way. Ramon, not wanting a fuss, took my mother's side. I felt utterly betrayed by him. It no longer felt like my wedding, but my mother's wedding. The one thing that really mattered to me, having Moira as my bridesmaid, was ignored. Mum saw only one drawback to the church wedding: Ramon and his family were Catholics and we were Protestants. 'A Catholic wedding *never*,' she said. As the feud continued I stood back, perplexed – if there is only one God, what were they all arguing about? At last a solution was found: our minister and Ramon's priest would conduct a joint wedding service in the Catholic Church. Apart from that, Mum thought Ramon was a good match. And she enjoyed telling everyone. Ramon was delighted to be the cause of so much pleasure. I hated Ramon and I hadn't even married him yet. My hurt and anger rose. I felt like a volcano ready to explode. Somehow, at that point, I should have found the strength to communicate how I felt but I took the only option I knew – anger. I was acting a part and I hated myself for my weakness. I felt alone, tired, and used aggression and bullying tactics to achieve my own needs.

I had begun to feel sick and dizzy. Nobody apart from Ramon knew I was pregnant. I was worried I would walk down the aisle and pass out, making a fool of myself in front of so many people. I was terrified that I would slump at the altar and faint, everyone realising my shame, that I was pregnant, and point accusing fingers at me. My mother had indoctrinated me into believing that it was wrong to sleep with a man outside marriage, and here I was, pregnant! The wedding day passed in such a haze that I wasn't aware of any of my actions. I couldn't drink, I couldn't smoke. I said nothing, but I did manage to smile. We went back to Balloch for our honeymoon, to the foot of Ben Lomond, the place where Ramon had been given the prediction and where Daryl's soul had come into the world.

I began to worry about the pregnancy as it dawned on me that something was growing inside me and moving. It was alive. I then began to fear its death. I would poke myself to check if the baby was still kicking. Was it still alive? I stayed awake at night, afraid there was no movement. I needed food to feed my fears. I couldn't take alcohol without throwing up so I turned to sweets and cakes, things I had never eaten much of before, and with this I gained weight. I also had a passion for macaroni and I got heavier and heavier. I ate two boxes of jelly babies a day, about six bars of chocolate and six cakes. I would tell the people in the cake shop, 'They're not all for me, I'm having friends round.' I ballooned from seven and a half stone up to thirteen and a half. I couldn't fit into any of my clothes. I even had to go into hospital because I had such high blood pressure. I just ate and played Pacman on the computer all day, the game where the wee man runs round and gobbles up the gold nuggets. I became a recluse. I didn't want anyone to see me and I didn't want to see anyone. I felt too big to go out, too fearful and ugly to be with people. I was depressed.

After the honeymoon we moved into Ramon's flat which was above Ramon's snooker club. He had used it as his bachelor pad for entertaining his friends, but had never lived there. He had lived at home where he was looked after by his mother. That was what he thought a woman's role was, to look after her man. It hadn't occurred to him to do anything to get the flat ready for us, since in the meantime we had bought a house which was being renovated. Why renovate two homes? But the flat didn't have a cooker, just a microwave, and the heating was utterly inadequate. It wasn't the best place to begin our married life. I was frustrated and took it out on Ramon, picking petty arguments. As a result, I saw less of Ramon. He would go out at ten in the morning and come home at midnight. Basically, he went back to his old lifestyle.

We were in his flat throughout the winter waiting on the entry date for our new house. With Ramon away all day and most of the evening I was lonely. I got lost in the computer, lost in the chocolate, lost in the cakes. I was 27 and I had no idea where my life had been or where it was going. It felt as if it was out of my control.

I thought if I could just give birth everything would be fine, yet nothing could have been further from the truth. The minute I gave birth, the horror started. I was in labour for 21 hours before Daryl was born. They had to cut me to get him out; I was screaming my head off. I really thought I was going to die. The minute I pushed it was extreme agony. Eventually I said to the nurse, 'If you cut me once more with those scissors, I'll stick them up your arse!' So I held Daryl in because it was too painful for him to come out and then he had problems with his heart. It was quite a drama and after I'd finally given birth, I threw up. In fact, I threw up all over Ramon. That served him right, I thought.

The first thing that entered my head when I saw Daryl was, 'Oh my God, Ramon's shrunk!' He looked just like a miniature Ramon, it was incredible. When they gave me my son I screamed. I couldn't bear the contact. The pain, the stitches, the indignity, the heat, they were all unbearable. They had to call a doctor in to stitch me up because they'd made such a mess. I couldn't even sit down for two months never mind have sex.

Ramon sat and joked with the nurses and I got no attention. Everyone came to see Daryl. I cried a lot. I couldn't feed him because I was in too much pain. Nobody seemed to see me or care; they only saw Daryl. He looked nothing like me and I couldn't believe this was my baby. The only one who talked to me was Dad. He saw my pain and hopelessness and gave me a pan drop sweet, patted me on the shoulder and told me everything would be fine.

Chapter Twenty

I was convinced that something dreadful was going to happen to Daryl and I slept with one eye open. I truly believed he would die because everybody else I had loved had died or been taken away. My blood mother was taken away from me and then my adoptive mother died. With Brenda, although I had a very insecure bond, there was also some love and she nearly died. I had instinctively known when Aunt Martha was going to die, my friend Gillian died when I was 21 and I now knew that my father was going to die. My reality consisted of anybody I really loved dying. I wondered, 'Am I worthy enough? Am I allowed to love? Will I be punished if I love?' Therefore I was afraid to love Daryl.

My confusion, fears and anxiety for this little ball of life deepened my depression. My lack of knowledge about the most basic care, like how to bath him, especially when he wriggled and squirmed out of my hands, triggered my eating problem again. I stopped eating and nobody noticed. I cried and cried; I felt like pulling my hair out. Nobody asked what was wrong. They saw me crying but nobody seemed to care. They put my behaviour down to post-natal depression. 'Women behave like that,' they said. But what was the answer? I didn't know and nobody else seemed to either.

Eventually Daryl and I came home from hospital to be faced with an untidy, cold flat. Nothing had been done. It was still winter and the flat was freezing. We moved the bed into the lounge for warmth but I was angry that Ramon had prepared nothing for our homecoming. If not for me, then surely for his son? I was living like this and yet still unable to do anything due to the pain of my stitches. We all went out with his mum and dad for Christmas dinner and I couldn't sit down; I couldn't speak, I was so depressed. Daryl was constantly screaming, he wouldn't sleep. When he finally did sleep, I kept one eye on him, scared that he would stop breathing, convinced that something would happen.

Motherhood was too much for me: I felt I couldn't cope with the responsibility. I watched Daryl all day and all night, waiting to pick him up and give him his food. My mother-in-law sometimes had him on a Saturday. This became the pattern of our lives and when we moved into our new house, she had him more and more. It was a relief to have someone else to take care of him, yet the more I watched him, the more convinced I became that something really was the matter. Nobody listened to my fears. He was seven weeks old.

One morning there was a desperate call from my mother-in-law to say they were bringing Daryl round, he was ill. He was very hot. I called the doctor. As soon as she saw Daryl she asked for tepid water to bring down his temperature and suggested he had meningitis. Fear gripped me. We bundled him into the car and drove him to the hospital.

Ramon was frantic. We were all frantic; mother-in-law, father-in-law, Ramon and me. To add to the drama, Ramon's mother had called the priest who arrived at the hospital and, without consulting me or Ramon, gave Daryl the last rites.

The hospital told us it was definitely not meningitis, but they thought he might have a urinary infection. Daryl had some tests and sure enough, the hospital's diagnosis was correct. And still I felt there was something else. Daryl was to stay in hospital for another week to get over the worst of his infection. By the following Sunday he was no better – he was seriously ill. I knew now that I had 'seen' something more.

That Sunday we found Daryl on a drip and a specialist at his bedside. He said that Daryl was bleeding, he had no blood clotting mechanism. He had been vomiting and passing blood and now he was on a vitamin K drip in an attempt to clot the blood. If it didn't work he would need to have a blood transfusion which, with a baby that age, was always very difficult, so we were looking at a seriously ill baby. Fear gripped me and I prayed incessantly. I told God that I'd do anything if Daryl would just live; at that point I would have sold my soul for Daryl to live. I think it was in this crisis that I returned to God. From time to time I had gone to church when I was in London, but really my spiritual life was largely forgotten. I still had a belief, but this had been obscured by drink and a fast lifestyle. I had made no space for another way of life. It was through Daryl's illness that I found a way back to God.

Eventually we were told he had the clotting mechanism and would not need a transfusion. Relief ran over me. Nevertheless, I could still 'see' that something was wrong – I could see that his stomach was getting bigger. Monday passed. On Tuesday I noticed the measuring tape round his stomach. I didn't need to measure, I knew it was bigger. On Wednesday morning I asked Ramon not to go to football, but he went. I came back home for a break from the hospital. The phone was ringing. It was the hospital. Daryl had to have an emergency operation. I went straight back. I had to sign the consent forms. He was anaes-thetised. I was on my own. I couldn't contact Ramon as I didn't know where he was. I waited and waited. Eventually, I went home. They were not clear at the hospital when the operation would be over but when Ramon arrived home we called the hospital for news and were told that the operation had been successful. We drove in straight away. Daryl was by now in intensive care. He was on diamorphine, and drips seemed to be coming out of him everywhere. To see a baby so small with so much equipment around him created more and more fear in me. I was horrified and I didn't know how to cope.

The next day I couldn't face going in to see Daryl, so I waited until the following day and was amazed to see the difference. There he was, smiling and moving and looking much better. My heart sang and I thanked God.

When I brought him home he had one enormous long stitch across his abdomen. I was scared to hold him, feed him, move him, but slowly I became more confident. Still the flat had had no changes made to it and I was cold and ill-equipped. I became depressed again. I wondered when the four-hourly feeding would stop. I was tired, so tired. I was worried. I watched him. I wondered how well he actually was. Even though I knew he was okay, I was left with my fears – every sneeze sent me into a panic.

At seven months Daryl began to walk. If I'd been less fearful as a mother, I might have taken pride and been excited that Daryl could walk so early. But instead he terrified me; I was afraid he was going to confirm my worst fears. He was naturally curious and continually exploring and touching things. He pulled things on top of himself, put things in the video, put his fingers into the electrical sockets. He got out the knives and plates, stuffed the telephone down the toilet, turned on the taps and flooded the flat. He even ate poisonous plants and ended up, yet again, in hospital. Although these were normal enough things for children to do, because of my intense fear of Daryl's death, I lived on my nerves, drinking and smoking to excess.

At mealtimes Daryl would push his food away so that every meal became a trial. My fears about my own eating patterns came into play. I got over-anxious about his not eating and probably persisted too much. I was scared that if he didn't eat, he might die. When Ramon was a baby he didn't eat, or drink milk, and Ramon's fear was that Daryl would not be tall. On a subtle level, then, there were a lot of fears surrounding Daryl that were based on Ramon and his babyhood, and on my own eating problems.

My mother's cousin George, who was 36 years old, committed suicide. When I arrived at his funeral I saw Mum, but Dad was not with her. I instantly felt that something was dreadfully wrong. Dad had been ill for two years now and had undergone several tests and a heart operation. Despite the success of that operation I knew all was not well. As soon as the service was over, I found Mum and asked her where Dad was. In an off-hand manner she told me that he'd been taken to hospital the night before for more tests and suggested that I shouldn't visit him outwith visiting hours. I told her I had a bad feeling about Dad's condition and that I was going to see him there and then. 'You're overreacting as usual,' she said. I raised my head and looked directly at her with defiance and walked away. Daryl's baby-sitter finished at one o'clock and this left us little time to get home, but I knew that if I wanted to see my father alive I would have to go immediately to the hospital. When I told Ramon my belief that Dad was going to die, he shrugged it off; but after much argument he agreed to take me to the hospital. When I arrived I met the doctors who said they were not too concerned about Dad and showed me into his room.

As I entered the room I saw my father lying in bed, propped up against some pillows. The light pouring through the window behind him seemed to be illuminating him. There were no audible sounds and yet it was as if I could hear music. It was an amazing experience. My father seemed to be surrounded by a grey haze of energy as if time stood still and then he smiled, saying 'You've come, my little girl, I knew you would.' We shared a beautiful silence which was eventually broken by myself uttering the words that I would look after my mother. He asked if I meant just for that night and I suddenly realised, as he did, that it would be for a lot longer. I wanted him to have his peace and I left the hospital saying my silent goodbyes to him.

I pleaded with Ramon not to go to his football game that afternoon as I knew Dad was dying and I wanted to be with him, and not looking after Daryl. Ramon took Daryl to his mum's. I phoned for a taxi. Just as it was arriving, the phone rang. It was the hospital. Dad was to have an emergency operation and could I contact my mother. I rang Mum, and went straight to the hospital but when I got there Dad had already left for theatre and the doctors told me not to worry. I left the hospital with a heavy heart. I collected Daryl and went straight to Mum's house. While we were sitting in silence, the phone rang. I knew it was the hospital to tell us Dad was dead. I put a bottle of milk to Daryl's mouth which poured all over his face and while he screamed uncontrollably, my mother's face confirmed Dad's death.

My Dad was the only stable thing in my life since my adoption at six months and I looked up to him because he was the wise old man. He could always answer my questions. 'Why do the stars come out at night?', 'Why does the kettle boil?' I once asked him if I could borrow £5 and he said no. I asked why, and he said 'What are you going to do when I'm not here? You're working, but you're not budgeting your money. Learn to budget your money because if you don't you're going to be in trouble. If I give you money it's not teaching you anything.'

There was also that time when I smashed my radio in a temper and Dad refused to mend it because, he said, I'd punished myself by not being able to listen to my music and it was a valuable lesson I'd never forget. He was right, I never did.

My father and I were linked in an unspoken, telepathic way. He was a wise man, he was creative. He drew fabulous pictures and seemed to be talented at anything he turned his hand to, especially the furniture he made for me when I was a child. He loved walking and the outdoors in general. This unspoken communication between us certainly made up for the lack of the physical. We shared glances and looks. He was so gentle that his true essence couldn't possibly ever hurt anyone.

I didn't cry when Dad died. Mum said, 'Don't make a scene. We just have to accept it.'

About two months after Dad's death, a friend was talking about having a get-together and asking a medium along. Intrigued, I joined the gathering at her house. The medium was called Mr Robertson and by the time my turn came I'd had a few glasses of wine, it was a party and all the girls were round. I really didn't think he'd come up with anything but immediately he said, 'There's a man here,' and I swung back on my chair thinking 'Oh yeah, this could be anyone.' The description began to sound like my Dad, but I didn't say I knew who it was. Mr Robertson went on to tell me what this man had worked at, what his character was like. I had gone along that night partly hoping I could contact my dad, but I wasn't honest enough with myself to admit it. Mr Robertson said, 'He's telling me that you don't know who this is, you're not making the connection,' and I said, 'Well, it could be anyone,' because I still wasn't going to tell him it was my dad. I thought 'prove it'. Then he said, 'He's getting a bit agitated and he's got something very important to tell you. He's now going to tell me how he died, because he's got a message for you. He's saying that he died on the operating table.' Immediately I knew for sure it was my dad. I stopped swinging on the chair and went blue with cold.

'Now he's got your attention and he's saying he's very, very sorry.'

'Sorry, what would my dad be sorry for?'

'He says he is asking for your forgiveness.'

Without hesitation, I said 'Of course.' But I didn't understand why he was asking for it. I wanted to know why, why? Then the answer came through: my dad was asking for my forgiveness because he had never stood up for me.

Even then I didn't fully understand; I still loved my dad, no matter what. He could do no wrong in my eyes. But this was an awakening for me, because my father must have been asking for my forgiveness for a good reason. It was the beginning of my recognition that Dad had weaknesses and imperfections. It made me see there was a huge gap between my image of him and the reality – that he had never defended me. I began to understand the difference between uncritical love and unconditional love. Unconditional love forgives without making judgements.

Chapter Twenty-One

When Daryl was 11 months old, we went to Florida in the US and took with us a nanny and a friend of Ramon's. Ramon wanted to leave Daryl behind with his mother but I wouldn't allow it. All I could remember was when my father married Brenda and left me when they went on their honeymoon. There was no way I could abandon Daryl.

There was an outdoor swimming pool at the place we were staying and we instructed the nanny that the door to the pool should never be left open. One morning Ramon's friend returned from a walk and took his breakfast to the pool. Forgetting the door, he left it open. The unsuspecting nanny thought Daryl was safely playing in the lounge. I heard a splash and instantly knew it was Daryl. I saw Ramon's friend diving in the water to pull Daryl out and I ran to help. He wasn't breathing. I carried his limp body thinking he was dead. Ramon told me to give Daryl the kiss of life but I didn't know how to do it and it was then that I suddenly heard my father's voice telling me what to do. I put him down and did what my father instructed. I gave him mouth to mouth resuscitation, listening to the details as I went. I felt I had entered another dimension. I managed to get Daryl breathing and his colour returned.

Ramon was banging his head off the wardrobe door in a gesture of helplessness. His friend called an ambulance and by the time it arrived Daryl was breathing but had hypothermia. At the hospital he underwent tests and proved to be okay. Daryl stayed overnight at the hospital, but Ramon blamed me, saying I should not have insisted on taking him to America.

Ramon had booked this holiday thinking it would bring us

back together. In a way we had both tried to use Daryl for our own ends: Ramon wanted Daryl to stay at home so that we could spend time alone and have sex again; I wanted to take him with us because it would make it easier to avoid sex. The irony of the whole thing is that Daryl nearly died because the very moment he fell into the pool, we were making love. I lived out my fear that if I didn't watch him, he would die.

Neither of us was able to discuss what actually happened, nor what we felt about it. Our separate guilts got in the way. To this day, Ramon won't talk about Daryl's near death. It's as though you just don't talk about the things that hurt you. There was no compassion between us, we were having a tug of war over what happened instead of recognising each other's pain and helping each other through it.

I felt I had let Daryl out of my sight and that was why he'd fallen into the pool. Ramon blamed me. At the slightest opportunity, he reminded me that Daryl should have been left behind with his mother. I believed him. 'Yes, it was my fault.' I was concerned that as a mother, I wasn't able to safeguard my child. I wondered why I couldn't have just left Daryl behind and gone to America and had a one-to-one adult relationship with Ramon in a beautiful place, free from worries, having fun. My self-esteem plummeted.

When we arrived home I decided to get a nanny, somebody else to look after Daryl, somebody else to take the responsibility. There was a spin-off. I now had freedom to go out with my friends and we drank and smoked and had a laugh. The drink numbed the pain and the hangovers gave me something to focus on. I retaliated with angry outbursts at Ramon, hating him for everything. We were drifting apart. Every time Ramon and I went out, he would ignore me. He would talk to anyone and everyone but me. As the only place we went to was Ramon's leisure club where he knew almost everyone, he had the advantage. Occasionally we would go to a restaurant but it was always the same story, there was somebody at the next table he knew and found more important to talk to than me. More often than not he would totally leave me out of the conversation and not introduce me, so I would order more wine and seethe.

The morning Daryl nearly drowned we had made love and

Tara was conceived. I was on the pill and we hadn't had sex for the whole 11 months since Daryl's birth. I remember lying in bed with flu and a stomach bug, symptoms I recognised from the last time, and I suddenly sat up and screamed at Ramon, 'I'm pregnant! I'm bloody well pregnant again.' I blamed Ramon. The horror of having to go through the pregnancy and birthing process all over again numbed my mind.

Chapter Twenty-Two

I began to work in Ramon's video shop and this gave me the excuse to keep the nanny to look after Daryl. If I was working in the shop, how could I also look after my son? I enjoyed buying the new releases, managing the staff, handling cash and talking to customers. I played the business woman and bought the appropriate suits for the part. Now I felt I was someone. I appeared to be the perfect wife and the perfect mother because I gave out that image.

When it all went well, it gave me a sense of my own importance, but when things went wrong, I was caught up in my anger and guilt. It was only too easy to take it out on Ramon; he was quite simply careless and charming. He relied on his charm but when things went seriously wrong, he disappeared from the scene leaving me to handle the fireworks.

One morning Ramon arrived at the shop to find two nuns searching for an appropriate film to show visiting nuns that evening. He charmed them, going through all the different films he thought they might like. At last they made their decision on a suitable film and Ramon decided to serve them himself. The next day two irate nuns came into the shop demanding to know who Ramon was – he had given them a blue movie instead of *The Sound Of Music*! I could only apologise and reiterate the fact that he wasn't a pervert, he was actually my husband.

A friend of my mother's who lived a few doors down from her was selling her house and we decided to buy it. In the midst of the move we were also negotiating the sale of the video shop as we needed the money for the balance on our new house. The transaction was completed on the day that I was taken into hospital for Tara's birth. I was determined that this birth would be different. My contractions had been going on all day but I wanted to wait until Ramon and Daryl arrived before going to the delivery room. This time I didn't want any drugs. I already knew how painful giving birth was and I therefore accepted the pain and Tara was born very quickly. The difference in my attitude meant that I didn't repeat the trauma of Daryl's birth.

After Tara was born, Jane our nanny, a lovely girl, took complete charge of Daryl and Tara, and I, no longer in the video shop, was free to go on shopping sprees. These filled my time and helped me to focus on something other than my continued fears about the children's health. I found it exciting spending money, wheeling and dealing, always seeing something more to buy, until finally our three-storey house was complete. Bored, I then moved on to buying new clothes; clothes for me, clothes for Daryl and Tara, as well toys and books. They had more toys than anyone had ever seen. I didn't save, I used credit cards and spent every penny and more. When the bills came in, I didn't open them. I just handed them straight to Ramon. I didn't care. He believed that if he paid for a nanny and sorted out all the bills then everyone would be taken care of. This was his way of being a good husband.

My moods swung between highs and lows. The shopping sprees were an adrenalin kick, it was as simple as that. I could get a high just thinking about what I'd buy next. It was exciting. But these were material things, and once bought, I found I wasn't satisfied. Whatever I had bought would lose its glamour. Then came the inevitable low.

Now that the shop was gone, Ramon started a new business, this time making video films, mainly of weddings. It had been a hobby of his which he was now turning into a profession. He was like a child, stumbling over himself in his excitement. He would make mistakes because he had never learnt the art of being a cameraman, but he truly meant well, he really wanted to do a good job for people. Nevertheless, I took the blame when his carelessness resulted in someone's wedding day being produced in blue because he hadn't used the right filter or another with no sound because he hadn't plugged in the mike.

I could have left the business at any time, but I was getting something out of it too – it meant I could avoid looking at any of my own issues. It also filled the gap, it filled the hours, it filled the days and then I could say to my friends, 'You'll never guess what he's done now!' I thrived on Ramon's mistakes because it gave me conversation and I projected all my anger onto Ramon, when really I was angry at life. I was in denial of the root cause of my unhappiness and used the dramas to avoid it. I focused on him being in the wrong – it suited me for him to make all the mistakes.

One day when I took the children swimming I sat watching them, staring into space. The roof of the swimming pool was made of glass and as I looked up, I suddenly saw an action-replay of the dream I'd had the night before. My surroundings faded into oblivion and I was looking at a man, a painter, someone Ramon knew. Although I couldn't see his face I could see he was painting the outside of windows and then fell backwards through glass. An ambulance was called as his face was lacerated although the rest of him was none the worse for the fall. It didn't make any sense to me but I knew that it was a warning. That evening I related the dream to Ramon who thought it was nonsense, yet the dream still seemed to ring warning bells in my head. Ramon checked where his painter was working and found him painting the inside walls at his club. Exactly one week later, the painter started to paint the outside of Ramon's mother's house. As he was painting the back windows, he slipped and fell through the conservatory. Every detail of my dream had come true. These dreams were happening almost every night. I saw a friend's sister's unborn baby. I could see what he looked like, what he weighed and how long her labour would be, all of which turned out to be accurate and totally bemused my friend. I began to use my dreams as party pieces which had everyone enthralled.

Ramon, the children, the nanny and I took a holiday in Cyprus. The men there followed me and chatted me up, which was exactly what I wanted as it was a way of getting back at Ramon. It was like saying, 'Look at me, I'm gorgeous, you should think yourself lucky to be with me.' It was attention seeking with an element of negativity because I wanted to punish him: I wanted to make him suffer because I was suffering.

We were both out of our depth. He had been brought up by a

mother who was prepared to do everything for him, and suddenly found himself with a wife who was not. Yet I think in a curious way, what attracted him to me in the first place was the fact that I was different. He saw that I wasn't going to let him get away with things. I put him on his mettle. For my part, I was also attracted to his originality. He was charming and intelligent, a risk-taker, an entrepreneur, but he wasn't controlling in the way that other men in my life had been. I had to find other ways of holding his interest. Once married, however, things changed. What used to be a funny quirk of Ramon's now became a source of resentment and frustration. No doubt, he found the same with me.

Marriage and children put a very different perspective on things. You can easily walk out of a relationship, but it's a lot more difficult to walk out of a marriage with children. I knew if I really pushed it, Ramon's way of dealing with it would be to disappear, not to face it. He never confronted me. He paid the bills, gave me a job and paid for the nannies. He saw himself as a provider. From a very early age he had worked in his parents' business. His father had always worked, his mother had always cooked. That was the way of things and he expected to follow suit.

When we arrived home from Cyprus the tension between Ramon and me was enormous and now, looking good with my tan and feeding off the attention, I was delighted when a man called Paul, ten years younger than me, became obsessed with me. Harry was Paul's friend and Moira and I ended up in a foursome on our nights out. I made myself believe it was a coincidence that the men always ended up in the same place as us! At first it was exciting and gave me an enormous sense of power: now I had someone who was in love with me. I wanted to believe that we were like Romeo and Juliet, that it was my destiny to be with Paul. But I made sure Ramon knew nothing.

Paul was a lovely person and would have done anything for me. I knew if I had said, 'Paul, fly me to the moon,' he would have found a way. But I didn't want to leave Ramon for Paul. I liked my life. What I actually wanted was Ramon, me and the kids, together as a family unit. I think it's very important when you're about to get married or live with someone, to work out what it is you want and what you expect from the relationship. I hadn't done this. I thought life was like a fairy tale. You got married, the magic wand was waved and everything was fine.

Paul's obsession with me grew. He met my children, bought them presents and wanted to spend time with them. I took comfort from his caring and it felt good to have somebody who wanted me, but he wanted more than I did. He wanted to marry me and look after my kids. Deep down I knew I loved Ramon and I knew I didn't want to end the marriage. I was living on my nerves, not knowing who would see me and give the game away. I hated Paul, I loved Paul; I hated Ramon, I loved Ramon, but most of all I hated myself. I hated the lies: my children and I, my life and my marriage, were all out of control.

Paul finished with his live-in girlfriend and my guilt deepened. My fear of being punished by God increased. I was afraid I'd get cancer because of my smoking, or perhaps my kids would be taken away from me – something awful would happen, something was going to stop me behaving badly but I didn't know what it was. I valued the intrinsic sanctity of marriage and married people didn't have external liaisons because you took your vows in front of God. The relationship with Paul wasn't positive, it just fed my drama. It made me excited, it made me feel alive, it was an adrenalin kick. Naturally, I wasn't able to tell Ramon any of my fears and I wasn't able to finish the marriage. I prayed that somebody or something would make the decision for me.

I hated my life. I had no idea which way to go or what to do except get drunk and be angry. My disgust at myself deepened and I became more and more self-destructive, drinking and smoking excessively. Life was a blur. I knew how much I was hurting others. My children were out of control and I couldn't cope.

Chapter Twenty-Three

I had to find another distraction to focus on. Ramon was always complaining about the cost of the mortgage so when I saw another house which was cheap and we could buy outright with no mortgage, I decided to buy it. Wining and dining, holidays and men, clothes and toys, weren't giving me the necessary kick. A new house would do it for sure!

As soon as we moved in I began to feel a presence. I could 'hear' voices, doors opening and closing when nobody was there. One night while I was sitting in the lounge I heard the most spine-chilling screams coming from upstairs. My first reaction was that someone was trying to murder the children. I ran upstairs and when I entered Tara's room she was sitting bolt upright. Through the screams she told me that there was a man sitting at the end of her bed. I suggested to her that it may well have been the cat, but she adamantly refused to budge from her story that it had been a man.

Sometimes I would hear someone coming upstairs at night; I would hear the sound of a door closing and assume it was Ramon. I could quite easily hear footsteps coming up the stairs, walking along the corridor and stopping. I would call out 'Hi, Ramon!' and there would be no answer. Ramon refused to believe any of this, passing it off as nonsense, until one night he came home late and slept in the spare bedroom. To his horror he saw and felt the bed covers becoming indented as if someone were walking over the bed.

One night I came home and as I entered the house I heard what sounded like furniture being moved upstairs in the bedrooms. My first reaction was, 'What on earth are the kids doing now?', yet something felt quite strange. There were no voices. I ran up the stairs and, as I reached the top landing, the noise stopped. I looked in the bedrooms and Daryl and Tara were sound asleep; there was total silence. I went back downstairs and found the nanny in the lounge. I asked her if she had heard anything and she replied that she hadn't. However, the next day, a hysterical nanny arrived at the video shop. She told me that as she approached the lounge, the heavy glass sliding doors shut in front of her, and as there was nobody else in the house she was terrified.

Things moved. You could put something down, turn your back and it was gone. It was constant. We also had so many fires that someone even said, 'You'll be getting Christmas cards from the fire-brigade soon!' One night I cooked chips for the kids and I know I put the chip pan off. I also switched the cooker off at the wall which I always did. The kitchen door was made of glass and after we'd finished tea, Tara said 'Mum, there's a lovely orange glow coming from the kitchen.' The place was ablaze. My lovely new, white, kitchen was ruined. It was black. By the time Ramon arrived I was standing at the front door in my pink leggings and pink fluffy slippers with a cigarette in one hand and a brandy in the other, all the windows open to let the smoke out. He couldn't handle it and just drove off. That was the last straw. I knew we had to get away from this house before something awful happened.

Chapter Twenty-Four

My mother Anne and I kept in touch after her move to Canada and one day she called to say she would like to come over to see me and the kids. There was no hesitation: I offered to pay for her flight there and then. I wanted her to come because her visit would be something else to focus on. While she was away, I continued to live the fantasy, seeing her as the wonderful mother, in all her wisdom, who loved and adored me. However, I also knew that the moment she stepped off the plane, I would turn round and look at her and think, 'I don't like you.' And that's exactly what happened.

Anne was only 15 years older than me so that when we went out everyone said, 'Oh, is this your sister?' and it made me feel quite good to have a mother that looks like a sister because she's young and vibrant. I could go drinking with her and tell her anything because she would understand, because she was the same as me, she'd had a lot of different relationships and had known emotional ups and downs. I thought that if anyone was going to take my side it would be her. She would understand and probably agree with everything I was doing, which was what I wanted to hear: I wanted someone to sympathise and not criticise me.

I couldn't have told Brenda about my marriage problems because she thought the sun shone out of Ramon regardless of what he did. How could I say we were having problems? I wanted to love Ramon, but I didn't know how to.

Anne had said she wanted to come over to see me and the children, and in part that was certainly true; but the part that she didn't mention was that she wanted to come and see her friends. She wanted to go out, get drunk and have fun, and that's what she did. When she arrived she was only with me two days before going off to Perth where she stayed for about a week. It was her almost immediate departure which awakened me to those patterns in her behaviour which I'd begun to notice just before she had left for Canada. There was a hardness, there were incidents of 'who gives a shit', and I saw a side of her which used others. At the time I was unaware of my own hardness, but nowadays I know that the surest sign of my needing to look at something in myself is when I don't like it in another person.

While she was with me I was dutiful and attentive. I fed her; I drove her around; I did everything she wanted; met all her needs. But I also had my own agenda.

I wanted to know who my natural father was. Anne wasn't keen to reveal anything: at first she pretended she knew nothing about him. However, I insisted. Now she told me, 'He was no good, he was a drunk, he never had a job.' I persisted. How could she know so much about a man who had raped her all those years ago? There was more to this than met the eye. Finally she told me his name. Bill Moran. I looked in the Perth directory and I found a B. Moran at an address that Anne recognised. I phoned him. I was blunt. I said, 'Do you know Anne Porteous?'

'Yes,' he said, 'I remember her.'

I said, 'Well, I am her daughter – does that mean anything to you?'

I babbled on about Anne being home from Canada and that I had only met her for the first time a few years ago. He sounded very confused but wanted to see me that night. Immediately he took my number.

I borrowed Ramon's fancy car, and my mother and I drove to meet my father in a pub. Thoughts were careering round my head. Who was he? What was he like? Did I look like him? Looking back, I wonder why she came with me because as it turned out, there was good reason for my mother not to have come. Even on the way to meet my father, she told me he would try to kidnap my children.

As soon as I saw Bill I could see myself in him. I scrutinised him, looking for similarities between us. I also saw a pained man, hard, yet caring. I was wary and didn't know what he was going to tell me. Here was another piece of the jigsaw being put on the table but it didn't fit. He had a lovely voice and as he told his story, he warned Anne first that he would tell the truth.

'I loved Anne. She was very young, just 15, when we met and I was playing in a band. I was ten years older than her and ready to settle down. Anne was young and carefree; she liked the attention from the boys. We went steady for almost a year and then Anne got pregnant. I know she told her mother I raped her, and I understand why she said that, but I want you to know that I asked Anne to marry me. I was told by your nana that they would have me charged with rape if I didn't leave her alone. I wrote them a letter saying I would go to church, I would do anything they wanted, but to no avail. My aunt then went to talk to them, asking if she could bring up the baby after it was born. The reply was "No, go away or we will call the police." I tried several times and each time I was told that under no circumstances was I to make contact again. My own mother abandoned me, I never knew my father and my aunt brought me up – so I knew the feelings of abandonment.'

After he finished, Bill asked Anne to confirm his story. She admitted that she had never been raped and also that she hadn't brought me up as Bill had been led to believe. I was so angry.

There and then I went to telephone my nana. I wanted verification of the truth. My mother and I finally left the meeting with Bill and drove home in a stony silence.

At the time I was numb.

I had already booked to go on holiday with Moira a day before Anne was due to return to Canada, so Ramon had to drive her to the airport. Anne took the opportunity to reveal to Ramon part-truths about my life, breaking my confidence. She suggested that I had had relationships with other men.

Ever since finding out about her when I was 13, I had built this image of the perfect mother, the perfect scenario, the fairy tale. It was my fantasy. When I met her at the airport I knew she wasn't a fairy-tale mother, and the realisation set up a friction between us. She felt it and retaliated. I had incurred her wrath because I had exposed her lies with regard to my father Bill, and now she was out for revenge. In truth, I think she also felt she had already lost me.

When I returned from holiday the nanny told me that trouble was afoot. I now had to face Ramon who, I discovered, had been questioning all my friends while I was away. He was raging. Faced with his accusations, I didn't know how to defend myself. I explained to him that he left me on my own too much and I needed more support from him, I felt abandoned by him, the children needed to see him more, I wanted us to be a family. He retorted that if he paid the bills, hired the nanny, gave me a job, what more could I ask for? Nonetheless he wanted to keep the marriage together for the sake of his mother and the children.

I asked him how he saw us staying together – because it would take both of us to change to keep our marriage alive. I pointed out that he was never there, he never shared meal times together with us or played the father role. His solution was to move to the country which would keep me away from the enticements of Edinburgh's night life. I asked what he was going to do to change his life but he said he wasn't going to do anything, that it would remain the same and I was lucky to have such a supportive husband, one who would forgive and still keep me as his wife. With a sinking heart, I finally realised that it was impossible for me to continue any sort of life with Ramon. I demanded a separation and a new chapter of my life began.

Chapter Twenty-Five

I found it very difficult to finish the relationship. I think I looked to Ramon as being my foundation, like my father – a pillar of security and stability – and in truth, I didn't want that to go, but I also knew I couldn't deal with Ramon staying. There was the issue of sex, too. I didn't want to be treated like a hotel when he came in late and wanted sex. My needs weren't being fulfilled. But it didn't mean that I didn't love Ramon. I just didn't know what I wanted. I didn't want to be on my own, I didn't want to be with Ramon, I didn't want *not* to be with Ramon.

One day I was at the hairdresser's when I heard about Ramon's new bachelor flat. This was a surprise to me as we were still living under the same roof. Should I pretend to know? Did everyone know we were getting divorced or did they think it was for his girlfriends? Angry and hurt, I confronted Ramon who looked embarrassed. He admitted that he did have a new flat and said that he would move out. It was two months before he went and only then because I had met Jo.

Jo was a musician and we were immediately attracted to each other. I saw a lot of him and Ramon knew it. When it was Jo's birthday, my friends and I decided to give him a surprise party at my house so I asked Ramon to move out before the party.

Jo smoked marijuana, as did most of his friends, and I joined them. Now I was both stoned and drunk. Being a musician, Jo's hours were different from mine. I changed my lifestyle to be with him, staying up late and getting up late and, as a result, the children suffered. They became uncontrollable. I let them do what they wanted as it was too much of an effort to stop them. I had no interest in life and became pregnant by Jo, but miscarried almost immediately.

I felt the need for something radical to happen, and the only way I knew then of making it happen was to move house again. I chose a house exactly the same as that of my parents in Kingsburgh Road. I think what I was trying to recreate was something I once had – it's always the same, the grass is greener on the other side. In our house at Kingsburgh Road there was Dad, Mum, Shuna and Patsy. There was a stability, a foundation. Even though I had a difficult relationship with my mother, somewhere I knew there was another side to it. She had been a mother, no matter what, and there was stability. This much I knew. Mother, Father, me. My choosing a house just like Kingsburgh Road was like going back to my roots and I believed that the house would create the stability and inner fulfilment that I so lacked.

I decorated it just like Kingsburgh Road. I bought the same much-admired lamp, an antique with gold material hanging down. It cost me a fortune, £1,000. I wanted the room to reflect that opulent mode. I had gorgeous red curtains with gold trims that matched the shade. It didn't matter how beautiful the house was or how much money I spent on it, the inner feeling wasn't there. The exterior was lovely but I never achieved what I was after. It was a show house and didn't give me what I wanted, namely my dad back and the family unit. The house was a front, a mask. Who was behind the mask? Someone who was desperately trying to find love, to create an atmosphere that incorporated all these things. Yet within the house I was still lonely, still searching, still looking for something. I still thought in those days that I could do it through material things – I didn't understand I had to do it internally, that it's not what you buy or put into a house, it's what you do, what you create within yourself that matters.

As the builder and I were going through the new house, I heard my name being called. Without hesitation, I turned round and there, at the top of the stairs, was an elderly lady. Suddenly everything around me faded, leaving just a grey-like energy. I only saw a part of her, the top part – I didn't see the stairs, the wood or the carpet. It was as if I was in limbo, held in an atmosphere of grey energy. Although her words weren't audible, I understood what she was telling me. 'There are going to be difficult times ahead, but I will be here looking after you.' Then, just as suddenly as I had been in the greyness, I was back, taking my next step down the stairs. By now the builder was at the bottom of the stairs but I still hadn't moved. The builder stared at my blank expression and asked me if I had heard anything he had said. I replied I hadn't.

I became obsessed with the notion of having a white fluffy kitten. The Cat Rescue found one matching that description. When I saw him, I immediately thought he was ill. I watched him, and even although he looked well, I still believed there was something wrong. I took him to the vet who said he was completely healthy and gave him his first injection. Within two weeks the kitten began to show signs of weakness so I took him back to the vet and was again told that there was nothing wrong with him. He became more unwell and I went back to the vet who this time said, 'Give him plenty of water.' Completely helpless, I watched the kitten die and yet an inner belief persisted that his life could have been saved. I was heartbroken, not just for the kitten, but for the hopelessness of the situation.

It was the death of this kitten which triggered my breakdown. I woke up the next day with my heart racing. Jo looked at me and told me to look in the mirror: the hair on half the side of my head had gone grey, which sent me into a total panic. I was sure I was going to die. I went to the doctor. Doctor after doctor could offer no rational explanation for my increased heart rate. Only when I had turned over every stone did I give myself up to God.

At last I touched on how immensely unhappy I was. I had tried to bury it by every means possible: by power over men, by my power of authority, my power of revenge, by extravagance, by drinking, dancing, smoking, reeling and raving. I had tried to whitewash my feelings of depravity with a white fluffy kitten which had died. Only when I truly reached rock bottom, when there was not one ounce of strength left in me or avenue to flounce up, or dead end to pit my weight against, only then did I finally break down.

I cried. I didn't eat. I didn't get out of bed. Waves and waves of panic and fear washed over me. I hated myself. I hated the way I couldn't say sorry. I hated the way I couldn't speak to the children. I hated the way I couldn't cuddle them. I hated my anger. For all those years, I had said to myself that I could look after them, I could manage, I would do better. And all I could do was shout and scream at them. They were far better off with a nanny.

I looked at my daughter, Tara. So pretty, all dressed up in her ballet costume, make-up done, hair combed. Why couldn't I have done that for her? What right had I to play mother when I was such a mess? I was constantly angry with the children. I knew I could no longer live like this.

Each in their own way responded to the situation. The children went wild. They screamed and yelled and I buried my head in my pillow. The house was a mess. Nothing got cleared up, washed, tidied. The more I shouted, the more they shouted back. Ramon, now concerned, brought me pizzas. He saw I had lost a lot of weight. Jo bought me a book about nervous breakdowns. And what did I do? I threw it away. How dare he say I was having a nervous breakdown! How dare he! That only happened to people who were psychologically ill. Why had he bought me this stupid book? Eventually, I sneaked a look. I flicked through a few pages. It was a shock to find the symptoms described in the book matched my own. This set me thinking. What was wrong with me if it wasn't a nervous breakdown?

In the meantime I continued to eat hardly anything, and I was losing weight fast. I couldn't go out because I was scared I'd never make it to the end of the lane. I was scared of people looking at me. I couldn't visit friends in case I collapsed and had a heart attack on the floor. In short, I blocked the whole external world out. That left me with virtually nothing to do except stand transfixed, desperately trying to keep a hold on the everyday working of my brain so I could keep some sort of control.

The doctor now visited the house. After one visit, he called an ambulance. He suggested that I might be suffering from food poisoning which seemed to be confirmed as I threw up violently on the way to hospital. Once I was in hospital, I stayed there for four weeks. They continued to test me for food poisoning. Ramon brought me my TV and the kids came to see me, but nothing seemed real any longer. I felt I had entered another world. I felt completely alone.

Tara brought me a beautiful letter. In it she told me how much she missed me and loved me. This was a turning point. Her words touched my heart. I hadn't realised the children loved me. I cried and cried and cried. She had given me something to live for again: my children. I saw her and Daryl as part of my life, not separate from it. The nurse on duty saw my despair. She asked me, 'What would happen to a wastepaper basket if you kept adding rubbish to it?' These words of wisdom touched my mind. Weakly, unthinkingly, I replied, 'It would overflow.' She smiled, saying, 'Think about it,' and left. I did. And there were more tears.

In all my time at the hospital, I had one other visitor besides my near family. The friends whom I had wined and dined, whom I had kept amused at my own expense – they no longer visited me. When the minister came, I turned to him as my saviour. Just when I was beginning to reassess myself, here was God sending me his messenger. I tried to tell him something about the mess I was in, fumbling for words, through my tears. Just to have someone to listen to me and not to judge, that's what I needed. The minister left, mumbling something about seeing my own minister, but I didn't have one. Despite, or perhaps because of this, I began to draw strength from my own inner resources. True, I was in despair, but one thing I knew and had always known was that I was different. I was unique. Knowing my uniqueness, allowing it to be my strength, not my weakness, was the healing I needed. I was like my little wild black kitten, Patsy. I had healed her. The power that was in me to heal Patsy was in me to heal myself. I also had faith in God.

I took a few more false turns and starts before I really found my way and I was still collapsing, sometimes scarcely able to breathe. Ramon persuaded me to go through the horror of having a 24-hour heart monitor attached to me. It was only after this ordeal that a diagnosis of panic attacks accompanied by depression was finally offered me. The doctor put me on beta-blockers and suggested I see a psychiatrist. I was still very resistant to the idea that I, of all people, could be suffering from anything so weird. Like many people, I saw a hint of mental instability as a road to the madhouse. I had a fear of 'mental' disorder. When at last I was referred to a psychiatrist, I was terrified lest it meant that Daryl and Tara would be taken away from me. I wondered if they would lock me up in an asylum and throw away the key. I went, however, desperately anxious to stay in control, to show him that I was well. It didn't work. I burst into tears the moment I entered his room, and I cried incessantly. Imagine my astonishment when he told me our appointment was over. All I had done was cry! I hadn't told him anything much. But he said I was all right: crying showed him that I was in touch with my emotions.

He was telling me I was okay. Somewhere in that statement I drew strength. If a psychiatrist was telling me I was well, there must be something in it. Part of me was not well, but if there was a percentage, no matter how small, that was well and I was sane, then I had to try and build on that.

I went to my mother's for four days and just sat. I sat in a chair and stared out of the window. The children came with me. I sat quietly watching my mother and the children. I saw her get angry with them but I didn't have the energy to react. It gave me a new insight: I could watch her with the children and see how she interacted with me as a young child. My exhaustion gave me the necessary distance. I could stay out of the way. I needn't get angry back. But I could see that what she did to the children, I did too. I got angry. I could see how generations might pass, and my child would do to her child what I had done to her. This was all at a distance, as if I was not there, the part of me that needed to slough its skin and the part of me that needed to emerge.

One day Ramon brought my car round to the front door. There it was, parked outside the window, taunting me, almost speaking to me. Drive me! Pick up your freedom! Memories of when I was healthy and could drive anywhere I wanted came flooding back. Slowly, very slowly, I made a decision to come out of the circular world of blackness. I took the first step. It needed all my strength, but I did it, and I drove myself home.

ABOVE: My adoptive parents, Maude and Charles, on their wedding day. Brenda, Maude's bridesmaid, is on the left

LEFT: At Applegarth, my first home with Maude and Charles

Maude and I betray a distinct lack of affection

Brenda, whom Charles married
shortly after Maude's suicide

With my only childhood friend,
Shuna

Wild child: if only I'd known then what I know now

My wedding to Ramon, 1982

With Charles.

Ramon and me with baby Daryl – this is the face of my depression nobody ever saw

ABOVE: My two children, Daryl and Tara

RIGHT: Tara, aged ten, at a David Icke exhibition. She set up her own table to draw auras and had people queuing up to see her

My natural father, Bill

Two trusty companions, Aurora *(left)* and Candy *(right)*

Scenes of the area
surrounding the
Natural Healing and
Spiritual Development
Centre at Auchen-
dinny, Roslin Glen

Part Four

Rebuilding

Chapter Twenty-Six

I was home again, but I still had a long way to go. I had no energy, I didn't want to go out, I took little interest in the children. For days and days, I would lie on the sofa, watching the TV, staring into space. Every Thursday the *Herald and Post* was delivered and I used to scan it, looking for things to buy. Glancing at the advertisement pages through habit, an advert loomed out at me, jumping off the page. It was for aromatherapy. *Aromatherapy can help!* it said. Fascinated, I looked closer at the list of ailments it could treat. I had never heard of aromatherapy but felt sure it could help me. I called the number immediately. A woman called Brigid answered and said she could see me the following week. 'I might be dead by then,' I replied, but she said calmly, 'No, you'll be fine, just make sure you keep the appointment.'

A week seemed too long to wait – I was desperate – so in the meantime I made an appointment with a hypnotist. I searched the Yellow Pages and chose the one with the biggest advert because it looked the most professional. I was very nervous but on arrival I was glad to see he had a smart office and all the accreditations. It meant I was safe, I wasn't in some quack's place. He was business-like and wrote down facts about my life. He then proceeded to hypnotise me and as I relaxed, I began to see myself at the age of four, at the time of Maude's death. After I came out of the hypnotic state I had no answers, just questions. Why had I gone back to that day? What was the significance? It wasn't what I'd gone for. I thought I could be hypnotised out of having panic attacks, just as you can be hypnotised out of smoking. Well, it didn't happen.

The appointment with Brigid finally arrived. I found her to be a normal, kind and caring woman who made me feel relaxed immediately. She listened to me and asked questions, taking a genuine interest in my story. She explained the process of nervous breakdowns, panic attacks and how the beta-blockers worked. She said they were helping to regulate my heart rhythm.

After a few meetings with Brigid I began to take an immense interest in her work. It was the beginning of a new life for me. I believed God had shown me an opening, He had given me a key and I was determined to unlock the door to my own healing process.

It felt as if I'd come out of a fog; there had been a black hole, a vortex with me spinning at its centre, and now I was coming out of it. I began to see how I had been on the run all my life, like a convict convicted of what, I didn't know, but forever moving on so as not to have my disguise uncovered, always hoping that the next move would provide an answer to all my problems. What I completely failed to see all this time was that I was running away from my emotions and fears. Now I needed to face them. I began to make the connection between my panic attacks and Maude's death. The healing process was beginning.

I was introduced to the concept of Inner Child work. This encourages you to draw and paint, often with your non-dominant hand, which in my case was my left. For the first time since I left school, I started writing, drawing, painting and reading. I began to see the positive qualities in myself and I began to like myself. I was changing. I stopped the destructive patterns in my life. I no longer smoked marijuana to get myself into a state of oblivion where everything was magical and wonderful. I didn't get drunk any more; nor did I have the same friends. I was in a process of rebuilding. It was as though I had suddenly awoken.

This awakening of the soul is not a sudden thing. It doesn't happen just like that, over a month or over a year. It's progressive, it's still going on and I'm still learning. It's a long journey. Just when you think you know it all, you fall, and there's only one thing to do – pick yourself up and learn from it.

The start of my healing process was the nervous breakdown.

Three months of oblivion. I didn't know where I was and many people told me they didn't know where I was either. I had no emotions, I acted like a zombie. If you'd given me a £1,000,000, I would just have left it lying there. I was in a huge vortex of nothingness. But in that nothingness I found my spirit helpers: I heard their voices giving me the choice to live or die. I wanted to live.

During one of my appointments with Brigid, she used a weighted object suspended in her hand to pick out aromatherapy oils for me. This was my first introduction to dowsing. Intrigued, I wanted to know more about how dowsing worked. How did a swinging pendulum tell you which oils to use? I was brimming over with questions. I looked at her books and longed to read them and understand more, desperately wanting to do what Brigid did. I asked her how I could learn more about natural healing and she replied that she was holding a course at the weekend. Without giving it a second thought, I enrolled.

But when I left Brigid, my enthusiasm left me. I felt I had failed at everything – I was no good and this was probably just another of my whims. Why on earth had I committed myself to this wretched course? My heart rate began to increase, I paced up and down the floor, and I worried. I thought up a thousand excuses to drop out, but in the midst of it all I heard Brigid's calm voice and I knew that she would gently chide me for all these self-made obstacles. Things would work out.

Everything fell into place. Daryl and Tara were being looked after and I was free to go. I had no excuse. Then I started to worry again: I worried that I would be late, that no one would like me. Would I like them? Would I be able to concentrate? What would I do if I had a panic attack? When I arrived, I looked around the room at the other faces and they seemed to be full of confidence, while I was shaking inside. We had to introduce ourselves and everyone seemed to have something interesting and intelligent to say about themselves. When it came to me, I barely managed to say my name and that I had two children. Brigid looked at me with a smile, as if to say, 'There's a lot more to you than that.'

During the course my thoughts wandered, waves of panic swept over me. Anyone who has suffered from panic attacks will know how strong a force it is and how it takes you over. I couldn't focus on what she was saying, nor could I understand much or remember anything about the aromatherapy oils. I was frightened, too scared to open my mouth to ask questions, scared in case I knocked something over. My hands were shaking and my mouth was trembling. I wanted to cry. At lunch time, I made my excuses and ran outside and smoked three cigarettes, one after the other.

When I returned, everyone was eating. I put a small amount of food on my plate and sat listening intently to the conversation around me. I realised how interesting these people were, how kind and caring; when they looked at me they spoke softly and included me in their conversation. They asked nothing from me and my head began to rise, my eyes meeting theirs. I was fascinated by their stories of spirituality. They were so enthusiastic that I had a million questions I wanted to ask. Their knowledge captivated me. I felt I could communicate with them because we had so many shared experiences. At last I had found like minds, I wasn't alone after all.

After lunch we began to practise dowsing but I couldn't get it to work. Everyone else's pendulums moved. I began to panic. I tried to concentrate. I even wondered if Brigid had actually been moving her hand all along. Just as I was about to give up, I saw my pendulum move. It seemed to have a life of its own. I focused my attention further on what was happening. I needed to programme in my 'yes' and 'no' responses so that when I asked questions the movement would indicate the answer. For me, the pendulum moving in a clockwise direction indicated a 'yes' while moving back and forth indicated a 'no'. Then I dowsed for a massage oil for my mother. The answer was no. Confused I asked Brigid why. When I told her that my mother had heart problems and had had a blood clot, Brigid said, 'You never massage anyone with heart problems.' Something had stopped me making a mistake, but what was it?

I borrowed a book on dowsing and became so engrossed that I read it right through that night and finished the book in time for the next day of Brigid's course. We made up aromatherapy oils specifically for ourselves by dowsing, then practised massage on each other using our own oils. I had left my massage oils in another room, so my partner used the oils she had made up for herself on me. After my massage I couldn't keep awake and curled up in a corner to sleep. Brigid was concerned and asked what oils I had used. When I told her I'd used my partner's, she asked her what she had made her oils up for. 'Insomnia,' she replied. Here was another lesson and proof of the accuracy of dowsing and the power of the oils. I slept very peacefully for the next few days, feeling tired, but happier and more relaxed than I had been in a long, long time. I wanted to learn more, borrowing more and more books from Brigid, amassing knowledge on the different aspects of natural healing. Book after book jumped out at me. My appetite for this new knowledge was insatiable.

One day I was dowsing over my vitamins which were lying in a drawer and the pendulum gave me a clear 'no' response. I was confused by this, it didn't make sense. However, I picked up my vitamins and saw the beta-blockers underneath and dowsed again but I got the same response. My heart knew then that I had to stop taking them. I knew intuitively that beta-blockers were wrong, and now my dowsing was confirming what I had never dared to ask. What was I to do? They had kept me alive, these beta-blockers, they had kept my heart stable, they had allowed me my freedom. The doctor had told me that in no circumstances was I to come off them, so what should I do? I was confused, fearful that if I did come off the drugs I might have a panic attack and revert to my old ways. I kept dowsing, asking for an answer. It was still 'no'. I knew I had to trust, and my own interpretation of the truth was that the beta-blockers were no longer any good to me. I didn't know what their side-effects were, I only knew I had to throw them away.

I began to follow my own path, dowsing for essential oils, Bach flower remedies and nutrients. I knew these would all help me. I put together a programme of natural remedies to replace the beta-blockers, taking bits of information from one book or another, bringing together my new-found knowledge.

In my enthusiasm I booked another course with Brigid to learn reflexology. Reflexology didn't appeal to me as much, but I felt compelled to book onto the course in any case. On the day of the course the other eight people who had paid their deposits didn't turn up so Brigid dowsed to see what we should do. After going through numerous different therapies she dowsed colour and got a positive response. Brigid then got out all her books on colour, to which she got a 'no' response. Confused by this she suddenly remembered the coloured bottles she'd bought from an exhibition the week before. When I saw the jewel-coloured liquid in the bottles my eyes lit up. I knew that this was what I had been searching for all my life. Tears came to my eyes – the joy, the relief! I felt like I'd come home. All my childhood memories came flooding back, memories of the fairy colours and how much they had helped me. Now, in seeing this colour, as if it were alive, I felt that I too had become alive.

We worked with colour and dowsing all weekend and on the Monday I phoned the company that had produced the bottles of colour to find out about their courses for training. They asked what qualifications I had and my stomach hit the ground because I didn't have any. So they asked me to write a letter with details of why I thought I should be allocated a place on their course. This triggered all my childhood memories of not being able to write very well and not being able to spell. How could I possibly write such an important letter? I sat down and prayed and began to write. I disappeared into myself and it wasn't a question any more of what I would write and how I would write it – it was written. It was an incredible letter. A new guidance was present, and I truly felt that I had been helped. I put it in the post box, not knowing what to expect.

I was now on a mission to live. I knew it would be a challenge, that there would be pitfalls; it was frightening, living on the edge of the panic attacks, knowing how easily I could slip back but I was filled with excitement. I knew then that my life was changing.

Chapter Twenty-Seven

I received a reply from Vicky Wall, the originator of the bottles of colour, saying I had been accepted on the course. Immediately I began to panic. Negative thoughts careered around my head. I was really ill. I was still having panic attacks and each day was a struggle. How was I going to travel? Who was going to look after the kids? Yet when you're meant to do something, a way will open up. My father, Bill, whom I hadn't seen for some time, suddenly phoned me and I blurted it all out: 'Bill, I've been very ill and I need to go to this place. I can't tell you why, but I need you to look after the kids – will you do it?' He said yes, and from there everything just flowed.

My friends said, 'Och, you're going to a hippy commune, you'll be brainwashed; it's a cult and you won't be coming back.' On the train to Lincoln, their words were circling around in my head. I wondered whether I was mad. Nobody understood how I could just up and leave for a bottle of colour, and neither did I.

When I arrived at the station in Lincoln I could see others who would be on the course by their colourful clothes. We began to gravitate together, pinks, purples, blues, all of us making the statement 'We are colour'. On the bus to the Dev Aura Centre we had endless things to chat about and suddenly my eyes opened, I had things in common with these people and I felt I belonged.

As it turned out, however, I almost didn't stay on the course at the colour centre! On arrival, I was taken to my accommodation which was a very old, tattered caravan in the garden. I looked at it in disbelief. This course was costing me a fortune and here I was, already an outsider, stuffed away in some old caravan. As a child I felt I always missed out if something was going on. This was how it felt now when I was the last to be given accommodation and was finally shown to this old caravan. As I pulled the curtains open a lot of enormous spiders fell out and I ran.

I desperately wanted to do the course and decided that there must be a reason I had been given the caravan for living quarters, even if I couldn't see it yet. In fact, it brought out the gypsy in me. Part of me, forgotten in childhood, loved to be alone, loved having the freedom to roam. The caravan gave me a sense of freedom and I felt I had come home. I could spread myself out and relax. I found myself sharing it with a girl called Jane, who was a spiritual teacher from Glasgow. We immediately hit it off. People would come for tea to our caravan and it was great fun. These were special tea parties for me: it was as if my childhood tea parties with the fairies and Mrs Rose had come alive in my adulthood. We talked freely about spiritual things and the caravan was full of colourful energies.

I didn't meet Vicky Wall, the course director, until the following day when the course began. She was dressed all in white with an amethyst stone necklace on a silver chain. Her hair was very grey and she had a beautiful complexion, hardly any lines, despite the fact that she must have been at least 70 years old. Her skin was like a child's. That was one of the most startling things about her. There was something very appealing about her, she was very knowing and had an extraordinary magnetism. Although she was blind, she seemed to know you if she passed you.

Vicky Wall was a person very much in her own space. She was the seventh child of a seventh child and I think she came into life as a very evolved soul. She was Jewish and very wise, obviously having studied the spiritual teachings of the Kaballah. She was a story-teller and all her teachings came directly from her own experience. I found it so easy to visualise her teachings as she told them. For the first time, when I met Vicky, I felt I had found someone who understood me at a profound level.

At the time I had a very strong wish. I wanted to stop smoking. Every week I would try, sometimes stopping for a couple of days or a week or two, but something always happened, giving me the excuse to start again. When I saw the bottles of colours I prayed, 'If colour is for me, if I have a future in it, I will stop smoking.' I dowsed out a coloured bottle, clear over violet, to help me. Unknown to me I had chosen the addiction bottle. I applied the liquid to my neck and thought, 'Let's see what happens.' The next day, in the top of the bottle appeared what looked like a cigarette end. Startled, I took the bottle to the course. Everyone agreed with me, except Vicky, who said, 'No my dear, that's the state of your lungs!'

At break I lit a cigarette and found to my astonishment that I couldn't put it to my lips. I felt sick and disgusted at the smell. I repeated the process at lunch time and had the same reaction. I have never smoked another cigarette since.

As the days passed, some of the others on the course were struggling with painful emotions that were surfacing: they cried about one thing or another and I found it a real eye opener. Why weren't they happy in such a wonderful space? I loved the course, loved being there. I looked at myself and thought, 'You've just had a nervous breakdown, yet you're clear and focused – so maybe at the end of the day you're not as bad as all that. You're not a nutter, you're not that ill any more.'

I was, however, about to learn a very important lesson. Just when I thought I was coping well, my first spiritual lesson arrived to show me otherwise. I got drawn into a vortex of negative energy which left me unable to cope with the course the next day. I was exhausted and crying uncontrollably. I felt as if I had been possessed by a demon. Vicky realised I was missing and came to find me, offering healing and words of wisdom. She told me that I was still open and vulnerable to other people's energies and I had picked up the negativity of others, making this my own. I realised I had so much more to learn.

During the course we learned about the overall language of colour. Vicky taught us what the colours meant, how we communicate with colour and what the healing properties of colour are. We learned about frequencies and energies, the vibrational aspect of colour and what can be achieved through colour. Vicky picked a pansy, a lovely indigo-coloured flower and put it in a solution of vodka to show us the colour moving from the petals into the liquid. The pansy turned white. However, when we returned after lunch, the liquid had lost its colour which confused Vicky until one of the students said they had been giving someone hands-on healing beside the bottle. Vicky explained that the energies of the colour had obviously been involved in the healing session. I kept an open mind and stored all this new knowledge in the filing system of my brain.

Vicky was an intuitive, wondrous woman and a special peace came over me when I listened in awe to her teachings. With colour, I had found my way forward. After I left her course, my interest in colour deepened, along with my own self-awareness and intuition. My aura wasn't depleted and congested any longer by the cigarette smoke.

At home I began playing with colour and learning more about the uses of the bottles but I never imagined myself as a therapist. I was doing this for myself, to help me on my journey to health. Brigid suggested I visit a medium called Alison who was also involved with colour, and much to my surprise, Alison told me that I would soon become a colour therapist, that I was very gifted and that one day I would create a healing centre; of this she was very sure.

Gradually people began to ask me what I was doing. Jokingly, I would ask them to choose colours but to my amazement, I found that I could unfold their personal story from their choice of colours.

I then had a vision of a small shop and, within a week, the shop I had dreamt about had a 'To lease' sign put up. It was just down the road from my house and I applied to rent it. Once the lease was finalised, however, I somehow got side-tracked from doing colour readings and turned the place into a gift shop, selling soaps and bubbles. My coloured bottles glittered on a revolving stand in the window but I was convinced that I wasn't ready to work with people. I was scared that God would take away my new information and that my spirit helpers would leave me. In time, I realised that I wasn't using the gifts I had been given. When I eventually did get started, my first client arrived almost immediately. I prayed and prayed that my spiritual helpers would be there and I was thrilled and amazed when the person I had done the reading for heartily thanked me for my help. I was stunned.

I had another dream in which I saw the shop transforming

into a clinic where both Brigid and I worked. I approached Brigid and asked her if she would be interested in my proposition. I was overjoyed when she said she was looking for somewhere new to practise as she had just sold her house. We renovated the building and soon the clinic was set up. It was called 'Good Health For All'. My colour readings were the talk of the area.

I continued with my own healing transformation, learning more about natural remedies, keeping to my own natural health programme, writing and drawing, keeping off drink and the drugs. Finally, I turned my attention to my relationship with Jo.

Jo and I decided to go on holiday hoping that it would improve our relationship. While we were away, I had a vision of owning a red dog, a large red dog, like a golden retriever. I heard a voice telling me to go out and buy the *Scotsman* newspaper. I looked up the column for pets and was drawn to an advert for an Irish setter. I phoned the woman and told her I would like to have a puppy. She told me she was in Aberdeen, which was miles away. I promised to be there the next day and when I put the phone down I suddenly wondered, 'What on earth is an Irish setter? Is it red?' Feeling rather stupid, I called the woman back again and told her that I wanted a red dog and the woman said, 'Yes, Irish setters are red!' and I knew that something special was happening.

We travelled to Aberdeen and arrived at the puppy's house to be greeted by two enormous dogs and several wild puppies. My wild self felt drawn towards the male who was intent on trashing the house, but I was beginning to listen to my son. Daryl sensibly wanted the quiet female with doe-like eyes. We set off on the long drive home and argued over a name for her until at last, the puppy had a name – Candy.

Candy was a quiet, soft, calm-looking puppy. She was wise and intuitive too and I loved her. But she did have a tendency to run off. She particularly liked to run across the main road to the butcher's shop on the other side. Of course, I was terrified. It reawakened all my old terrors of my children dying. But I was also learning. In the past, I would have confined Candy to the house and made her a prisoner of my own fears. Instead, I began to examine my hatred of cars, the noise and pollution they cause on a busy main road. It stirred in me the gypsy-longing for the countryside, to be somewhere peaceful and quiet, away from the fast pace of city life. It triggered in me a childhood memory of playing at farms: my farmyard was one of my favourite toys. Without knowing it, the seeds were being sown for a move to the country.

Candy's teachings were far-reaching. When she did something bad I would really vent my anger on her, but she just sat there, head down, cowering. I would also shout and bawl at the kids. Eventually, I saw the sadness in Candy and that penetrated. Because she couldn't talk back when I shouted, it gave me enough space to realise what I was doing. Whereas the kids would shout back and create a whirlwind of energy, Candy's silence and love gave me space to see what I was doing. When someone is angry and if there's a space to see it, you can diffuse it. Because of her wisdom, I was able to break the cycle with the kids too. She taught me about love and she took on much of my negativity. When I lay in bed, she would lie as my pillow. She was always there; we trusted each other. She was faithful and loyal.

Candy was good for my physical health too and we walked up Corstorphine hill every day. I was being re-connected to beauty and nature. With each step I took I said aloud, 'I am well. There is nothing wrong with my heart.' I listened to my heart rhythms and felt the difference in my heart rate from a slow to a fast walk. As I began to know my heart rhythms, I began to let go of the fear. I did this walk every morning, without fail. I also recognised the negative chatterbox in my brain. I told it to shut up – I was only going to hear positive thoughts. The power of doing this day in, day out was immense. Each day I prayed and became a little stronger, gaining more confidence and knowledge. I was taking control of my own life. I had found the real me. I was taking time to get to know the children, talking to them and learning from them, putting down boundaries. I let go of my expectations and my anger and we came together naturally.

One day my mother took Candy for a walk and when she came back to the clinic, Candy collapsed. Immediately I

stamped her foot demanding to go back outside, laughing and saying, 'Told you so, Mum.'

I told Vicky about the Good Health For All clinic I shared with Brigid in Edinburgh and about my colour readings, and over the week my confidence began to grow. Vicky asked me to present a talk to the 36 people on the course. I felt my heart race. My old fears re-emerged and I panicked. As she called me out to the front of the class, I slid further down into my seat. 'Come here, my little Scottish girl,' she said, 'now is the time for you to talk.' Reluctantly, I moved to face the class. She held my hand and told the group, 'Alison is too frightened at the moment to talk. Her heart is racing, so I will hold her hand until she calms down, because in the future she will talk to large groups and she needs to remember my energy around her.' Holding her hand I felt the power of her being enter mine and slowly I began to melt into her and she into me. My heart rate calmed down and Vicky announced that I was ready. All the faces were looking at me. She had known the moment was right. My mind was blank. I had no idea what I would say, yet as she held my hand I could feel her peace and her knowledge fire through me. I spoke to the group and didn't remember what I had said, but I saw the rows of faces suddenly looking intrigued, leaning forward in their seats. When I finished talking they all applauded. I had done it. I have never let go of the feeling of holding the master's hand in mine, giving me understanding and empowerment. It was a spiritual victory. I knew that from then on, I would never be alone.

Before I left, I had my talk with Vicky. She told me that I would create my own colour system. She said that I was always to believe in my own inner truth and never go against my own beliefs. We exchanged a wondrous silence and I knew this was the last time I would be with her and we parted with love. She handed me her precious crystal pyramid with the words 'Success Through Change' inscribed on it.

When Jo and I arrived home I faced up to the fact that our relationship was going nowhere and that I couldn't stand to be around what I now saw as the negative energy of his cigarette smoke. I had to find people who understood my spiritual journey. Sadly I realised we had to part, and Jo left. On my own, I no longer felt alone.

Chapter Twenty-Nine

At a New Year's party I saw a man I was deeply attracted to. All my instincts told me to keep away, but I didn't listen to this inner wisdom. He was good-looking, he was a challenge, he was different and I wanted to flirt. I wanted a relationship. He fitted my new bill. It was as simple as that. If I'd met him before I wouldn't have been attracted to him because it was only when I was telling him about my work with colour, that I drew him in. His interest in me drew *me* in. James worked on the oil rigs in Aberdeen and on one of his visits home, he got my number and called me. We fell madly in love and he moved in with me immediately.

My old patterns of behaviour were still there. I needed the excitement of taking on impossibly challenging men. Despite the fact that life had opened a big door for me, I was still dependent on the flattery, the excitement, the adrenalin boost. I needed to be needed. I realise now that life is a journey of learning, it doesn't happen over night; but at the time I thought I was pretty cool. I thought I'd done all the necessary work on myself – and that this was a new stage, he was a new person who would feed me in a mature, caring, loving way. I only saw what I wanted to see. I didn't see him for what he was.

A part of all human nature is our being conditioned to believe that we need a partner, we have to have a relationship and a family. I say to people now, 'Be very careful what you ask for, you might get it!' The relationship had started in my imagination. I created the figure that I wanted: I wanted help with the clinic, I wanted somebody who would understand the work I did, I wanted a partner on the colour side, the physical side, the emotional side, and I asked for all that without putting in any of the finer details.

Despite having already learned so much and knowing what I didn't want, I still launched in, eyes half shut, when I saw this guy. He was the one who fitted what I had in my mind, the Romeo and Juliet image. That's what he was, an image. And it didn't matter about his other side – I ignored it, because I believed that love would conquer all. James could almost have been anyone.

He resented Daryl and Tara and wanted to control them. I should have seen it. He was showing all the signs of being that old possessive type of male, the kind I always seemed to let myself be attracted to. Yet I still continued with the relationship.

One day, I went out with James to buy a fridge when I heard a voice telling me to go to the property centre. I had moved house seven times in seven years and had vowed never to move again. But two weeks prior to this, James had asked me what I was going to do in the future and, much to my amazement, I said I would develop a Natural Healing and Spiritual Development Centre in the country. Today we were out looking for a fridge when the voices clearly told me to visit the ESPC, the Edinburgh Solicitors' Property Centre. I went in and looked around but was unable to see anything. Still the voices persisted. James followed me into the shop and walked straight towards a photograph of a house. It looked like a hut on a hill to me. It was in a place called Auchendinny. I'd no idea where that was, so I laughed when I saw the small, hut-like house and walked away. However, James took the particulars and once in the car again, the voices continued. There was a new force operating in me. 'Forget the fridge,' I said, 'Let's go to Auchendinny.'

Chapter Thirty

We looked at the map and found Auchendinny about ten miles to the south of Edinburgh and headed off, clutching the photo of the hut on the hill. As we drove through the gate into the grounds of Firth Lodge I felt as if I was being transported into another dimension. I got out of the car and breathed in the surroundings. The beauty engulfed me and at last I knew I had come home. In front of my eyes, in the car park, was an old stable block and as I looked closer I heard a voice telling me that I was to create a natural healing and spiritual development centre here. In that moment I could see the old stable block being transformed, as if I was seeing into the future. I could see a beautiful building, painted green with a red slate roof surrounded by lush trees and plants. It was alive with smiling people walking around looking happy and at peace. It was magical.

I felt I knew this place, as if it already belonged to me. As I walked further into the property I saw some beautiful plants and peony roses. They were stunning, so red and vibrant. The main house was vacant and I peered in through the windows. It was a mess inside but I could see a huge fire place. I loved log fires. When we went round to the back of the house, we realised that this was the side that had been photographed. The lounge had an enormous window onto a spectacular panoramic view across the valley. Horses roamed in the fields below while the viaduct on the right spanned the river. On the other side, a tree-clad bank rose, unfolding onto fields which rolled up to meet the horizon. The view was unbelievable.

The whole place had a wonderful energy. There was so much

to see: there was the house, the old stable block in the car park, a cottage, a row of brand new stables further down the dirt track and 21 acres of beautiful scenery. The viaduct belonged to the old railway and was now part of a walkway between Penicuik and Roslin.

The cottage was called Strawberry Bank. I loved the name. Strawberry Bank Cottage. It conjured up an image of tea and scones, with strawberry jam and double thick cream. I could just imagine the strawberry pots outside in the summer. There was so much space. I could see myself growing organic vegetables. My imagination began to run riot. What could I not do with so much space? The excitement took away from the fact that the whole place was an absolute heap and was falling down. Already I was seeing it through rose-tinted specs.

Here I was, face-to-face with my vision at last. Here was the natural healing centre. Yet fear got in the way: it would be the most enormous task. 'How the hell am I going to do it,' I thought. It would be such a huge change. The biggest change I could ever envisage. I was on the verge of changing my destiny. I knew the relationship with James wasn't working but I still needed the support of a man to get this project off the ground, to help me with this vision. I needed someone to do the physical work – that was what I saw as James's role. I couldn't do this by myself. I thought James was 'meant' to help me.

From the house there were some steps leading down the side of the valley with a gate at the bottom and as I went through I got the fright of my life. A donkey was climbing the steps. In an absurd way it reminded me of Jesus and the stable and confirmed to me that this was the right place. It felt almost like the Findhorn story in that you find somewhere to put your roots down and start to create something spiritual; and after that, there is growth and development. Yet, until now, it hadn't been something I had ever thought possible. It wasn't as if I consciously planned, 'Let's have a natural healing centre.'

The vision had come alive before my eyes. The next moment it had gone. I blinked. I had to buy this property, I had to transform the vision into a reality.

I sold the clinic and put my house on the market. At the

time, house prices were very high. I dowsed to see what offer I should make for Firth Lodge and got £138,775, considerably less than the asking price of £155,000. Having bought and sold seven properties in seven years, I knew the property market inside out. I always decided what offer to put in and what to value my house at, not what the market dictated. One time I bought a house for £62,000 and sold it for £125,000 within a year. When I saw this property I knew it had been empty for years; it was totally dilapidated. I felt that the offer price of £155,000 was too high. I also knew I couldn't afford that much. By this time I was dowsing a lot more and trusting in the answers. I believed that if I was to create a natural healing and spiritual development centre, then I would be given the right offer to put in. It wasn't just a case of 'Oh, well, let's move house'. I had been given a vision. To merely decide on the offer on an intellectual level without asking for guidance didn't feel right. I handed it over to a greater wisdom and £138,775 was the offer.

The main house of Firth Lodge had been empty for four years. It had a lot of damp and the roof was nearly coming away. It would be a massive undertaking. Strawberry Bank Cottage was indeed a dilapidated building with two bedrooms and a lounge. There were no cooking facilities, just a log-burning fire in the hearth. It had burst pipes and there was no toilet or running water. The new stable block was the only good building in the whole shooting match.

I was so confident of getting the property that I set about trying to find an occupier for the stables, knowing I would have to rent it out to help pay off the mortgage.

The day came for offers to be accepted. There had been no other notes of interest, so I saw it as a mere formality. But this was not to be: another offer, the same as mine but with a better entry date, came at the last minute. I saw my dream shatter. The estate agent called and said that he felt there was unfair play going on and if I would bring forward my entry date he would recommend I get the property. I did this and won. The house, the cottage, the stables, the land, were all mine. The vision could now become a reality.

While waiting for the negotiations to be completed on Firth

Lodge, the property market dropped and my house wasn't selling so I had to take out a bridging loan. I left this to my lawyer to arrange but as the final week approached, I realised it hadn't been done. In a panic, I called my lawyer who said he was struggling to find me the money. Two days before the entry date to Firth Lodge my lawyer called and told me I'd better put it back on the market.

I couldn't believe my ears. For the second time, I was about to lose Firth Lodge. I called Brigid, who had a spare hour to meet me. Brigid told me, 'Alison, it has to do with the Allied Irish Bank.' I looked blankly at her as she repeated, 'It has something to do with the Allied Irish Bank.' 'The Allied Irish Bank?' I kept repeating the name. It made no sense to me. How had I been given the vision to create a natural healing and spiritual development centre at Auchendinny, and yet not be able to buy the property? Brigid broke the silence, 'It's somehow connected to the Allied Irish Bank. Who do you know that works there? The Higher Management is telling me it is the Allied Irish Bank.'

Suddenly I remembered that a friend's ex-fiancé worked there. I had seen him by chance two weeks earlier in a restaurant and, not having seen him for two years, felt too embarrassed and shy to say hello, although at the time I had a strong feeling that I should speak to him. I called the Allied Irish Bank and asked if Michael Dwyer still worked there. He didn't. My heart sank. I asked, 'Do you know where he is?' and they replied 'Yes, here is his phone number.' At this point, I didn't know Michael Dwyer very well, or what he did in the bank but, fired up, I called him. I briefly explained the situation that I needed £139,000 in two days and although it didn't seem possible, I felt sure, somehow, that he could help me. He said he would come and meet me in ten minutes. I put the phone down. Brigid looked at me and said, 'You've got your money.'

Confirmation came two hours after my meeting with Michael Dwyer. The Bank of Scotland would give me the money. In two hours I had managed to raise £140,000. My faith and my understanding of the spiritual world deepened. As I reflected on the day, I saw the vision of the beautiful house and its surroundings and the future of Firth Lodge. I knew now that God wanted me to fulfil that vision.

I didn't realise it then, but many more miracles were to come. I was laying down the deepest foundations of my life, my roots, my spiritual home, my spiritual work, my spiritual development. It was a very long road, an amazing story of learning and trusting God – and myself – and of being with God; of meeting many people along the way and working in the service of God for others; of working with the energies and the spiritual helpers that God gave me. It was the beginning of the greatest change of my life. The difficulties I had to overcome tested my faith to the limit.

Chapter Thirty-One

James asked me to marry him. Mum was convinced that this was a bad idea, but no matter what she said, I knew best. Yet something niggled away in the back of my mind: I felt a need to protect my property. I insisted that James sign a legal document denying him all rights to Firth Lodge. Mum paid for most of the wedding, which was held in Roslin Church in August 1991.

For our honeymoon we went on a barge holiday and on my insistence, we also took Daryl and Tara. The legal document I had asked James to sign cut him deeply and within days of our marriage he told me he didn't love me and wished he'd never married me. He also said he wished that he'd stuck to his vow of never marrying someone with children. This sent me into deep despair.

On our way home we visited a small seaside village and I was immediately drawn to a sign on a caravan advertising gypsy readings at £10. I couldn't resist. The gypsy began to relate accurate details about my life and the children's, but when I left I realised she hadn't told me anything new. So I went back to her and asked her to tell me something I didn't know. She replied, 'What is it you have wanted to do for a long time now?' I shook my head in bewilderment. At last she said, 'Write a book about your journey. It will be a paperback, written like a popular novel, but it will be spiritual. You will have help with writing it and receive confirmation of what I am telling you within 24 hours.'

The next day we drove back to Auchendinny and within five minutes of our arrival a girl called Anne arrived. Anne had come to the centre several times to take part in my workshops, but I didn't know her very well. We got talking and she said she was a ghost writer. Aghast, I told her my story about the gypsy and her prediction. Anne laughed and said she'd help me write the book. I agreed and we arranged another meeting.

While we were discussing the book, I told Anne about my natural parents, and the fact they came from Perth. Anne looked at me enquiringly, and said 'Does Bill have a son called Victor?' I said, 'Yes', to which Anne replied, 'My sister is married to Victor!' For me, this coincidence could only mean that Anne and I were supposed to work together.

However, I couldn't see the bigger picture, and in time Anne and I realised that the book was not the reason we had been brought together. So for the next few years the book was shelved.

In 1997 I held a workshop in Edinburgh on healing for animals and met Midi Fairgrieve, who was in the process of writing a book about natural treatments and remedies for pets. She and I kept in touch, and she used a photograph of Candy's pup, Aurora, and my cat, Mr Pink, for the front cover of her book. The following January we were talking on the phone and Midi said, 'I'm looking for another project to get my teeth into.' On hearing her words, the medium's prediction that two people would be involved in the writing of my book was ringing in my head. I told her I had the basis of a book, and that perhaps she would be interested in working with me on it. She took my first draft away and by April we had begun working together. I do believe that God works with precision planning. The time was right to start the book.

Chapter Thirty-Two

My house still wasn't selling and the entry date for Firth Lodge was upon me. I now had to pay for it. In an effort to stave off financial doom I rented my house out to foreign students, six at a time, and an artist friend of mine, John, looked after them, although I still cooked their evening meal. The day we completed on Firth Lodge, James, the kids and I moved in.

I managed to rent out the stables which brought in some money on a weekly basis, but this was constantly eaten up by the massive bridging loan. I had to pay £1,870 a month before adding on our food, heating and general living costs, and soon the debts grew. The woman renting the stables proved to be a difficult tenant and she and James took an instant dislike to each other. I found myself in the middle, trying to stave off the inevitable confrontations between them. I wanted peace at any price! But life has a very exact way of reflecting back to you the very issues that you need to deal with yourself. Their anger was my anger. My fear of their confrontations was fear of confronting my own anger. At the time, however, I felt it was best to keep the peace. After all, this was a spiritual centre and on a practical level, we really needed the rent money. Money was an on-going problem.

The children and I had been going to the markets every Sunday to sell off the stock from the clinic and the house. Bit by bit, furniture was being sold. Bit by bit, ornaments and possessions that I had once flamboyantly bought, had to be sold. One day at the market it had been raining. It was wet, drizzly, cold and damp and I felt very alone, frightened about the task ahead. A thousand thoughts ran through my head. We needed money for food. Why was I keeping Firth Lodge? What was I doing to the kids? Why was I putting them through this hell? Why were we living in these dreadful conditions? No wonder everyone thought that I was mad. Now even I was wondering what on earth I was doing.

I was exhausted with the undertaking of getting up early at weekends to go to market and cooking the students' food in Auchendinny and driving it into Edinburgh every day. Here I was at the market again, and for what?

Suddenly I heard a voice telling me to look down. I had become used to these voices and so I did as I was told. All I could see were puddles in the mud, then something caught my eye. It was a caligraphy picture in a brown frame, lying on the ground beside the stand across from me. It had the words: 'God shall supply all your needs.' I stared at it. All my questions had been answered. I realised that God could bring about miracles. I knew I had to have this picture. It was very old and tattered, but nonetheless, the message was clear.

I had no money and I waited and waited to see what I would sell. By early afternoon, I looked over to check if the picture was still there. My heart almost stopped. The picture was gone. I ran over. I asked the woman where the picture was. Had she sold it? She said, 'No. I believe it is for someone special and I've put it behind my stand waiting for that person to come and get it. I presume it is you.' I looked at her with relief. I said to her, 'I can only give you £4 for it. I don't have any more than that.' She took the £4 and gave me the picture. My spirits rose. I almost jumped for joy. Forgetting all the problems surrounding Firth Lodge, nothing seemed to matter except the picture. What a change from the days of spending £400 on a wooden unit with no significance. The picture now hangs above the fire place at Firth Lodge, having been restored and re-framed in 1997 by a local man, Archie, who had lost his wife and found peace here. I had told him the story of the picture and he restored it willingly, and today those words are forever preserved for people to come and read and I thank him immensely for the lovely job he did.

Chapter Thirty-Three

The following Sunday at the market, I was again questioning the prudence of hanging on to the vision of a natural healing and spiritual development centre. I still had no money, I was still paying for the bridging loan, I was tired of it all and ready to throw in the towel. I wanted to run away, to live abroad, relax in the sun and forget about everything. Then a very strange man appeared. I watched him approach. He had long, grey hair and he made his way directly towards me.

He told me he had come to give me a message and asked me to pick a card from his pack of colour cards. I was intrigued at once. How did he know that I knew about colour? He told me that I was not to go abroad to live. He said 'Absolutely *no*.' I had given him no information, I just chose the cards. He said I was to stay and that all would turn out well for me.

He told me he saw a wooden cart going down a dirt track with only one wheel. He said, 'You have to achieve putting all four wheels on the cart to balance everything up and once the cart has its four wheels, it will drive slowly and steadily. But the learning consists in getting the cart balanced. Until the cart is balanced there will be more obstacles – but each obstacle is also an opportunity for learning. It won't happen overnight.'

He described Firth Lodge – the house, the outbuildings, the surrounding land and the river – and he told me he had been sent to give me the strength and conviction to keep going with the project. If I didn't put the four wheels on the cart, I would have to come back and redo it. Then he was gone.

Many weeks later he reappeared. I was very depressed again

and wanted to give up. It was a very bad day. He said he knew I was disturbed over the property and that it was causing me financial stress, but life was going to improve for me. Already he could see I was putting the wheels on the cart. He described the spiritual energies surrounding the property and the importance of the herbs growing there. I thanked him and gave him some crystals and thanking me, he went on his way, with these parting words: 'Don't give up. The cart is on the track.'

One afternoon I was in a shop in the centre of Edinburgh when I suddenly felt impelled to run out. I had no idea why. I just knew I had to go, leaving the assistant looking bewildered. I ran down the street and when I turned the corner, an arm grabbed me out of the crowd. It was a gypsy selling heather. She said, 'I have a message for you.' Then she went on to describe Firth Lodge. She said that I was the one to transform its energies and that I was to stop worrying about the money: it would come. It was my initiation – I had been given something special to do and I was to keep going. She then blessed me and disappeared. I was stunned, shocked, amazed. I stood for a while staring into space, as if transfixed, and wondered where she had come from and where she had gone. I knew this was another miracle and my energies lifted. I was on the right path and God was keeping in touch with me in many different ways.

My bank manager decided that the bank could not help me any more: the bridging loan was still costing £1,870 a month and I was sinking further and further into debt. At this point my luck changed. The bank manager was replaced and we now had a new assistant manager, a Mr Brian Wallace, who began to look after my finances. He could really communicate with people and help them, and after we talked he began to see the situation I was in. He realised I had paid thousands of pounds of bridging in a year, but he didn't think the help I had received was the best they could offer, so he set about reorganising the whole structure. He became my financial adviser. I had someone to help me, someone who cared, and for a short period my finances had a reprieve.

So many times, the vision of creating the centre was almost sabotaged. It was at this point, with finances running out, that

I had a premonition that Ramon would buy my house, which still hadn't been sold. A five-bedroom, clumsily converted house. I could see that he would save me and buy it. I related this to Ramon. 'My Higher Management have told me that you're going to buy my house, how about it?' He was horrified. He said, 'We're not married any more. You're with somebody else. I can't bail you out. I've got my own life. My own flat in the West End. Why would I want to give up my custom-built flat for a five-bedroom house that I don't even like?' I said, 'Well, I'll just leave it with you.' I knew in my heart that I wouldn't have to say any more. I knew I had to trust. I knew God was saying 'Let go and let be'.

Somehow I let go of the fear and began to trust. But I still prayed to God that if this was going to happen, then please, let Ramon hurry up! That was November. The following February Ramon called me and said, 'I don't know why, but I will buy your house.' He put his flat on the market and had a buyer within a week. Brian Wallace had by now successfully sorted out the muddle of my finances. Ramon bought my house. Things were beginning to balance out.

At times of crisis, Ramon has always come through for me. He knows in his soul why he is doing something. He believes in God and one of the ways he expresses his spirituality is through financing this vision of creating a healing centre at Auchendinny. Something deep down was telling him he had to buy the house, not just for his kids, or for me, but for something much greater and much deeper than that.

I was now left with a much reduced mortgage of £90,000, but still very little income.

The builder at Firth Lodge discovered we could get a grant to renovate the property so we applied and were successful. In the process, however, the council condemned the house and we had to move into Strawberry Bank Cottage, still with no cooker, and winter looming. I had to spend some of the non-existent money to put in a shower and toilet. There was a small fire in the cottage which we used for cooking and we turned the lounge into our bedroom. At night we had to fill the kettle so that we could defrost the outside pipes in the morning and get running water.

Winter temperatures fell to -7°C that year. Ice covered the ground and James with his moods could not be guaranteed to keep the log pile stocked. It was a way of life that went out hundreds of years ago.

Chapter Thirty-Four

There was still very little money coming in, but I ploughed on regardless, my faith pushing me on. It was a busy time. I was running two houses, looking after the children, looking after the students, looking after the animals, renting out the stables, overseeing the work on the house, doing my colour readings and going to markets at the weekends.

On top of that I had a failing marriage. I began to see James in his true colours: he played games, sometimes staying away all night, not speaking but communicating only by letters, and then at other times he would not allow me out of his sight. Even going shopping caused problems for me. If I took longer than he anticipated, he caused a scene. He moved out. He moved back in. Life was a physical, emotional and mental roller-coaster.

I also began to see shortcomings in my colour readings and realised there needed to be a deeper level to my work. Having given so many people readings, I had become fascinated by the influence of the mind and emotions on the physical body, and its relation to colour. I had to do something more and I wondered what.

I got a book from the library on tarot, runes, stones and astrology. I didn't know it then, but I was naturally veering towards clairvoyance, mediumship and healing. The tarot attracted me so I decided to learn more about it and eventually designed my own pack in which I incorporated my knowledge of colour. To test the cards I picked one for myself. Its message foretold of a 'serious illness and hospital treatment'. I knew at once this related to me. The next day I woke up to find I had an enormous lump on my hand. It was red and swollen. I went to the doctor who looked at my hand and suggested it might be a bite. At that moment I felt as if invisible hands were lifting my jumper. It was like another force was lifting it up: I already knew I had a lump in my breast but part of me wanted to ignore it. I showed him my breast with the inverted nipple. He felt it for lumps but, finding nothing unusual, confirmed there was nothing to worry about. However, he wanted to follow procedure and arranged for me to go for an X-ray. I knew it was cancer.

When I returned home, I remembered that Ramon had kept up my private health insurance cover. I called the doctor to tell him I was with BUPA and he arranged an appointment the next day for a biopsy. The specialist who took the biopsy told me he was sure there was nothing to worry about as he could feel nothing. The results came back. I had a small cancerous tumour.

Cancer! I was devastated. The word boomed in my head. My whole world fell apart. Fear shot through me. I felt numb. I was assured it was a very small tumour but it didn't console me. Somewhere inside, I felt I was breaking. I felt alone. Although people came and went and said they were sorry, no one could feel what I was feeling. I cried and cried, as I had never done before. This was the biggest hurdle I had ever faced. I looked at what was happening to me and wondered why. Why was it happening and how would I cope with it?

I knew that I would have to rely on my faith more than ever and I used it to calm myself down. I tried to keep balanced, as balanced as I could, at least, in the circumstances. I allowed the tears to flow. I allowed self-pity. I knew what was happening to me – I just wasn't sure how to deal with it.

I knew now that my healing wasn't complete. I had a bum of a husband and I was living in the most basic conditions, following what seemed to be an unachievable dream; life was anything but wonderful. My thoughts swung between death and life. I could die from this cancer or I could live.

After the operation to remove the tumour I stayed in hospital for a while. I was being treated privately at the Murrayfield Hospital in Edinburgh. I needed some time on my own so I decided to stay in as long as I could, but my breast was also very painful, excruciatingly so. The surgeon, Mr Lee, came to see me every day after the operation until he could not understand why I was not going home. I told him about the excruciating pain. He examined my breast and when he put his hand over the area I felt an intense heat. It gave me almost instant relief. The pain was gone. I realised the healing power of this man. He wasn't just a surgeon, he was a healer. He did it intuitively without recognising what he was doing and I thanked him silently for the wondrous healing he had given to me. I was now ready to go home.

Later on I found out that as I was whiling away the hours in hospital, ordering food and running up a bill, believing the insurance would cover it, one of Ramon's managers cancelled the policy because Ramon had decided that he could get it cheaper elsewhere. There was a difference in the dates between cancelling the original policy and taking out a new one. Out of the ten years we had been covered by BUPA, this four-week treatment of two operations, hospital accommodation, nursing care, medications, meals and X-rays was not covered! Poor Ramon had to foot the bill which amounted to thousands of pounds.

There's no question in my mind that Ramon and I are bonded, soul to soul. After my operation the first phone call I got was from him. There's enormous support between us. Even now, people say they can see us getting back together. First he bails me out on a bricks and mortar level by buying my house, which enabled me to put down my foundations and fulfil the vision of a natural healing centre, and now he pays for my life. Had he not paid for my treatment I would have had to have waited at least another four or five months before I could be operated on, and who knows how far the cancer might have spread in that time.

After the operation, I had to decide what kind of further treatment I wanted. The hospital suggested I had chemotherapy and radiotherapy, as well as taking a cancer drug called Tamoxifen. They also wanted me to have my ovaries removed. It was a huge decision to make. In the meantime, I needed to find somebody who could help me, somebody who was medically trained and yet worked with natural remedies.

Over the years I had occasionally come across a woman called

Dr Muriel Mackay. She had done a wealth of research into diet and nutrition since the late '50s and I decided to call her. I told her of my situation and asked her for help. She immediately put me on a detoxification diet and some of the things she suggested seemed almost unbearable at the time, like drinking organic beetroot juice. She told me this would be good for my blood. I did everything she asked of me, unquestioningly. I changed to organic fruits and vegetables and built up a nutritional programme to help with the detoxification process. She knew my financial situation and knew I couldn't afford regular treatments, but she still agreed to see me and took nothing in return. She gave me faith and showed me great kindness.

In Muriel Mackay I found a depth of awareness and in her treatments I had an insight into true healing. I realised then what was missing from my colour readings: I could analyse people's emotions and find the root cause of their illness, but I couldn't take that further and treat them. In Muriel's system of natural healing, once a diagnosis had been reached, a programme could be specially tailored to individual needs.

During my first appointment with her, she gave me electro-crystal therapy, something I had never heard of before. Using a special machine which could read the subtle energies of the body, she scanned my aura to find out where my illness lay. She was looking for disease in my electro-magnetic field, which in my case had already manifested onto the physical as breast cancer. The treatment involved using high pulse frequencies from a machine through an electrode with saline solution and crystals to balance my energies. Muriel's treatment embraced many therapies: she was also a homoeopath, a nutritionist and a reflexologist. I benefited as much from Muriel's treatments as from her wise words, her compassion and her understanding.

Chapter Thirty-Five

By now, my good friend, Muriel Mackay, had arranged for me to see Harry Oldfield, the creator of the electro-crystal machine, on his first visit to Edinburgh. I told him nothing about my illness; he scanned me and told me I had cancer, and where it was. He said, 'My suggestion is that you have radiotherapy and take Tamoxifen, but you don't need chemotherapy or your ovaries removed.' I was amazed and delighted. His suggestion for my treatment confirmed what I'd already decided for myself. I was very impressed by his therapy and his insight into my condition.

Muriel insisted that I begin to learn electro-crystal therapy. I said, 'It isn't for me. I can't do it.' I gave her every excuse, but she held her ground. 'You *will* do the electro-crystal therapy training.' I wondered where I would get the money although I was too proud to tell her this; yet another part of me knew I would find it, if it was meant. I was afraid of taking on such an enormous subject, of working with a scientist, with Muriel. But Muriel saw. She knew better and there was no running away from it. I was doing the training.

This was the first electro-crystal therapy course to be held in Scotland and was run jointly by Harry and Muriel. Reluctantly, and feeling under pressure, I joined the course, having to sell more furniture to pay for it. I might add that it proved to be worth every penny. Harry's teachings opened up a whole new area of understanding for me and the people I met on that course are still true friends. We learned together, shared new ideas together; we met once a month for 18 months and as our knowledge grew, so did the bond between us.

For the next 18 months I continued to have treatment from Muriel and gave up doing colour readings to concentrate my time on the electro-crystal therapy course. I was fascinated by this new knowledge of subtle energies and auras, how to read them and what treatment to give. I even sold my precious John Lewis lounge suite to buy an electro-crystal machine. I learned how to interpret a person's life story through the colour of their aura. I learned how to use the electro-crystal machine to diagnose and heal. Life took on a deeper meaning, another dimension was opening up for me and I drank in every piece of information I could get.

We spent weekends at Muriel's house learning about her work. It was no good going in with the attitude that it was a talk and nothing more. We all had to participate. Muriel added her own dimension to the knowledge she was implanting in us and we all grew. Eventually the course finished and it was time to write the thesis. There was no help from Muriel in this. 'Get on and do it yourself, girl. You can.' And I did. I got my Electro-Crystal Diploma, with many thanks to Muriel.

I began to meet up with Muriel as a friend and we discussed case upon case. Her work was fascinating and her knowledge immense. She became a mother figure to me and I, like a daughter to her. I found her caring, wonderful, intelligent, knowledgeable and a pioneer in her field. She had no problem asserting her views and pointing out to people their errors, and when it came to speaking the truth, she was unequivocal. Her deep devotion to natural healing was with her at all times: she was always collecting information from all over the world, cutting out newspaper articles, reading books, keeping herself up-to-date with the latest remedies, whether it be Manuka honey or aloe vera. Her thirst for knowledge was insatiable.

Muriel had been a keen organic gardener since 1965 and had a great influence on Daryl's terrible eating habits. He thought it was quite all right to eat a Mars Bar before taking to the football pitch or filling himself up with Coke and chocolate cake. A child who refused vegetables, now, under Muriel's guidance, he was learning the essential qualities of healthy eating. He was growing, becoming stronger and more at one with his own being. Muriel helped Tara in many ways as well, and gave her an understanding of natural healing. She influenced many people's lives for the better.

Chapter Thirty-Six

There seems to be some correlation between women who have nervous breakdowns and then within two years of their breakdown have breast cancer. In numerous cases that I'm aware of it may not be coincidental, and I think if research were done on this we would find evidence to support it. The evidence might surely provide a warning for women who have suffered from nervous breakdowns in the past.

When I had my breast cancer the first thing that clicked into place was the answer to the question: 'What is this about?' I looked at my life. At the time I was in a lot of confusion. I was confused about my colour readings: I could tell people their life story and they would say 'How clever', which fed my ego. What I began to realise was that this approach was highly irresponsible. I could read a person's pain and trigger issues that they might not be ready to deal with and I didn't have the expertise to help them through their healing process.

I was also confused regarding my marriage to James. I was discovering that I didn't respect him. Somehow I had persuaded myself that if I counselled him, it would help him solve his problems, which in turn would solve the problems between us. Of course, the more I pushed, the more he resented it.

I tried not to get angry. There was an awful lot of stress. We were living in a very small, run-down, dilapidated building with no heating, no cooker, no proper facilities. While it looked all very well and good to me, it didn't to other people. They would say, 'What the hell are you doing there? You're living like tinkers and you've got no money, nothing.' Yet somehow I knew I had a lot – nevertheless I also knew things had to change, I just didn't know how.

As usual I thought I had done all the necessary emotional work on myself and gone through the understanding stage of why I behaved the way I did. I thought I was a relatively evolved human being, working spiritually, working for God. I wasn't. I had taken the skim off the milk. In fact, I hadn't gone into anything deeply.

Not long after my cancer, a family brought their 23-year-old daughter to see me because she was suffering from ovarian cancer. I had started working again, having trained with Dr Mackay and Harry Oldfield, and I felt I was getting my life back together. All I heard was cancer. In my mind I knew she had come because this was God now saying, 'You've gone through your cancer, you've learnt – now it's your turn to cure her.' There was no question about this in my mind. She came to visit me weekly and I put into practice everything I'd learned. I genuinely believed she would live, because she had come to me. She was also having chemotherapy treatment from the hospital. She was on a dietary regime, and my job was to give her electro-crystal therapy, but I mostly gave her hands-on healing because she just loved it and got so much from it. I was coming into my own and I realised 'this is what I am, I'm a spiritual healer'. Then complications set in and she went back into hospital where she stayed, and died. I was really shocked by the news. Her husband was a baker and had often brought me bread, so I had got to know them well. I had gone through all the issues with her; she had opened up and let go of so much that when she died I couldn't believe it.

It was one of the hardest lessons I ever learnt. We are not God, it's not our decision whether someone lives or dies and we cannot see the whole picture. Is it mapped out in the stars, is it in our Karma, is it our life's journey to go through certain things, who knows? But it certainly isn't for any practitioner to make that judgement. I had thought I was able to cure her, but I didn't have the understanding then. Now my understanding of the practitioner's role is that we are simply channels, and not here to resolve or invent anybody else's fate. I know now that God works in mysterious ways and people have their personal destiny which cannot be changed by us, regardless of what we want for them. We have the ability to help people on their way whether into life or death. Healing can help them on their journey, not decide what that journey is.

Having cancer brought me to the edge and opened up a new part of me, a feeling part. I got in touch with the part which had always felt hard-done-by, what I now call the 'Woe is me' syndrome. Whether I had or hadn't been hard-done-by isn't the issue, the important point is that this is how I felt. I felt I hadn't been listened to, I felt I hadn't been loved. Underneath all my bravado, all my cleverness, vision and determination, there was a poor orphaned being. Woe is me! But having got this far in my inner search, I had to go a stage further.

It was around this time that I met a hypnotist at an alternative health exhibition in Glasgow and was so impressed with his dowsing that I decided I should book an appointment. When he hypnotised me I went straight back to being aged four, the day Maude died. 'Here we go again,' I thought. I was in the lounge; I could see it and feel it. I could feel the anger rising in me like a volcano. All these years I had suppressed this anger. I was seeing red. Everything was red. The hypnotist then asked, 'What is upsetting you?' and I said,

'It's dark and I can't reach the light.'

'Why not just leave the room?' he replied. 'Just open the door and leave – what's stopping you?'

I realised I couldn't because it was locked and he suggested I try the window, but I couldn't reach the latch. Anger was mounting in me and he could see this. He said, 'You have the ability to open the window. You need to be outside.' Somehow I managed to open the window and once outside I saw lots of marigolds, a carpet of yellow and orange flowers. I felt calm and comforted. The colours were very significant: orange represents shock and trauma, but it's also comforting and creative, while yellow represents the central nervous system, joy and happiness. When I went for my appointment I hadn't expected to go back to the day Maude died. For the first time in my life I was angry at Maude for locking me in the lounge; I was angry at her for killing herself; I was angry at my dad for hiding the truth about her death. I had learnt at a very early age, the day I had thrown the brick at the girl who was taunting me, crying 'no mother' at me, that it was wrong to let this anger out. The lesson had been too strong and that's why I had learnt to hide the anger. I left the session with the hypnotherapist a transformed person. Getting in touch with my anger made a lasting difference to my life. I had been released from the trauma, I had moved on and got out of that room.

By getting in touch with my deepest feelings I was able to unlock the anger. I became so angry but this time I was beyond being analytical about it, I was beyond thinking 'I'm not entitled to be angry.' I unleashed this anger, usually in the shower where I would scream on my own. I would cry and howl like a child in a temper tantrum, banging my fists and then collapsing in a heap absolutely exhausted. I was finally in touch with my feelings. I went into this feeling space and asked Why? Why Me? Why me again? The difference was that I touched something in me that I hadn't touched before.

By experiencing the anger I felt seriously empowered, beyond belief. I had now found my true freedom. My God, this was real freedom. This was the beginning of my being able to sleep in a room with the door shut. Up until that point I couldn't even be in a lift on my own.

It was as though the floodgates had opened. The four-year-old child in me which had been locked in, was let out. I thought I had done my inner child work. I'd written out all my negative thoughts and feelings with my right hand. I had then used my left hand, the non-dominant hand, the feeling hand, to answer them. But I was still analysing although I didn't realise it. I really believed that I was doing the work, that it was enough to understand the negative patterns with my mind and enough to correct these patterns. But I wasn't feeling it. Why? Because it was too painful.

It was only at this awesome crossroads of having cancer that I finally realised that I hadn't done enough. The cancer grounded me and forced me to review what was going on. Inner child work does have merit, but the practitioner must take the client into the feeling state. I was very lucky with the hypnotist I saw, who not only took me into the feeling state, but also took me out the safe way. It's impossible to over-emphasise the importance of finding a practitioner who is able to take you through the early experiences in a safe and responsible way.

With the work I was doing on myself and my new lifestyle, I suddenly became happier than I ever remembered being and didn't even question why any more. No money, no facilities, very little food and masses of work, yet this lifestyle, just being able to walk out of the door in the morning and see the most beautiful sunrise and smell the fresh air, was something money could never buy. I felt at one with the world.

Chapter Thirty-Seven

By 1993, Firth Lodge was gradually taking shape – the walls were re-built, the roof was attached and each day I woke to see something different. As it began to change, the atmosphere lightened. The summer was hot and the flowers and trees were showing off their colour in glorious splendour.

Things were going very wrong between James and me. I swung between loving him and hating him. He tried to control me and part of me needed that. I so desperately needed to be wanted, and this control on James's part proved how much he wanted me. It made me feel special and created a false sense of having boundaries, keeping me safe from the world. The problem was that the boundaries hadn't been set by me, but by James's controlling behaviour. There was another part of me, the free-spirited part which rebelled at this control. How dare he stop me having my freedom? And yet, the more I rebelled, the more restrictive he would become. He was very jealous of me. He didn't like me having my own children and he didn't want me to relate with Ramon. He swung between being angry and nasty to me, to being loving, caring and sensitive, especially when I was ill. Then he would nurture me on every level. As long as I was down, he was up. The minute I was up, he pushed me down. Other people must have picked up on the bad vibes and learned not to call by.

Again I reached rock-bottom, wondering what on earth I had done. I saw my children's hurt, their father's pain and I blamed myself. Ramon had been good to all of us and he was being punished. He wasn't allowed to come to the house and if he did, the arguments and scenes got out of hand. I began to look over my shoulder. I had to watch what I said. I was living in fear.

We were heading for disaster. James restricted the children's freedom – even restricting their food – and slowly they changed. They began to distrust. They looked out of their eyes sideways. Daryl ran away from home numerous times. I couldn't understand James, nor could he understand me. He was full of anger and he was childish. Loving one moment; hating with venom the next. Lording it over the place, believing it was his one moment, and hating the fact that it wasn't the next. Working for short bursts and then accusing me of using him and treating him like a labourer. Life lurched from one drama to the next. There was no harmony.

James finally came up with the idea that we could start a pig farm – typically, he wouldn't even read a book about running one. For him, it was simply a way to be in charge. It was the issue about keeping and killing pigs that finally made me face up to things, squarely in the face. If this was a natural healing and spiritual development centre, it was obvious to me that there could be no killing of animals. Yet to James, this was quite incidental. It finally dawned on me that James's presence was going against my vision, my purpose in life. There was no way I could live with James and fulfil the vision. The two simply didn't go together. I finally had the courage to ask him to leave. And the moment I did so, my self-esteem blossomed.

In fact, James was delighted at my request and two days later I understood why. I received a letter from a solicitor, *his* solicitor! They were suing me for half of the property and half my car. I was shocked. I was scared, and yet I knew I had come a long way. I meditated; I prayed; I had loved and lost, and now this. I would be forced to sell everything I had so dearly fought to keep. I was determined that this wouldn't happen despite the fact that his letters and his lawyers frightened me. I couldn't think what to do. Although James had signed away any rights to my property before we married, it didn't seem to make any difference. I didn't understand why this was happening and for a while I didn't even ask my spirit guides for help.

The legal wrangle went on for two years. James got an

advocate and so did I. It was a game in which each of us played our part. Right from the start things had gone wrong. Then the woman who rented the stables left and I had no rental income.

The old 'woe is me' cry rose up in me again. I felt, once again, that everything was being taken away from me. But this time I had a greater understanding. I didn't have to fight back out of spite, just to prove myself, just to show I was a fighter. No, this time I knew to let go.

I knew I had to trust, to meditate, get myself into a space where my emotions were not taking over and where something could enter with clarity. I prayed for my spirit guides, and they gave me an answer, an answer that I was capable of hearing this time. I was still on the material level with my struggle with James, so they came in on a material level. They came in the form of Vicky.

Somewhere in the back of my mind I heard her voice urging me. 'He's unemployed, he gets benefit, he's on legal aid. Ask about that.' I couldn't understand why, but I decided I must ask my advocate. I told him,

'He's unemployed, he gets benefit, he's on legal aid. Does that make a difference?'

The advocate answered, 'Yes, if a person is on legal aid he is only entitled to a maximum of £2,500.'

Why had my lawyer not told me this in the beginning? Why had he put me through hell? Why had I been led to believe for two years that I might lose my house, my home, my centre, everything? I looked at the advocate and said,

'I don't want the court case. Pay him. Pay him and get the whole divorce and settlement finalised.'

My trust in my spiritual helpers grew even deeper. That same day Brenda offered me the money to pay James off. 'Get rid of him,' she said. The battle was over. Firth Lodge, the natural healing and spiritual development centre, was saved.

One Sunday in 1994 I decided to stay up all night to meditate and pray. I decided if something didn't happen within the next week I would put the property on the market. I was tired. I was angry. I was fed up. I had no help. I knew that something had to be done. The following morning was beautiful and I decided to dig the garden. Suddenly, I heard the doorbell. Armed with my spade, wearing wellies and my pink pyjamas, I answered the door thinking, 'Who the hell can this be on a Sunday and what do they want?' I opened the door and there in front of me was a woman with blonde hair, blue eyes and a large smile. She invited herself in and pushed past me. 'Do come in!' I said, slamming the door. My remarks went unnoticed. In an authoritative tone, she asked me where the coffee was. I began to see something positive in her approach. Coffee made, she said she was local and had heard of me and asked what it was I was trying to achieve here. I told her about my vision to create a centre but that I had had enough: money was non-existent and I really believed I had come to the end of my tether and would have to sell. 'Rubbish!' she said, 'get washed and changed, we're going out. I will introduce you to some people.' Well, I had said to God that *something* had to happen and here it was.

Joan's coming revived my belief in the vision and she infected me with her enthusiasm. She had a similar vision to mine and I felt that at last I had support – most importantly, it was local support. It made the centre more of a reality because people were beginning to hear about it. I was over the moon. At last all my problems were solved! All I needed now were a few helpers and I determined I would cast out my net and trawl.

Part Five

Good Health for All

Chapter Thirty-Eight

One of the first things I decided to do to pay off my astronomical monthly debts was rent out a room in my house. I put a notice in the local newsagent's and with this, Andrew arrived. Over the next few years I was to learn one of my most important lessons.

Although Andrew seemed a bit rough, his girlfriend was very pleasant and well-spoken, so I allowed him to move in. He said, 'It's a big place, you'll need some help. We could do an exchange.' I was so focused on bringing in money and getting the work on Firth Lodge completed that I turned a blind eye to his shadowy side and left myself vulnerable. At the time, the remaining work wasn't urgent, but Andrew, wanting cash for drugs and drink, would find jobs to do here and there. On the one hand, his behaviour went against everything I believed in, but on the other hand, I wasn't seeing clearly – I was caught in the trap of having no money and that's where I got stuck. I was expecting people to do things for me on the cheap because I had no money and so the energy was all wrong. Andrew was the first of many fish who slipped through my net, and so for a while Firth Lodge teetered on exchanging rent for work and having the dramas that went with it. In reality I still wasn't bringing in any money and I continued to allow the situation to go on.

Because of my desperate need to finance this vision, I let almost anyone in. I had no clear boundaries: I was only seeing the part of them I wanted to see. They could bring in rent money, help with the building work, help to develop the colour therapy course, and help run the business. If they had something to offer that I needed, that was all I saw.

A friend of Joan's slipped in because she was a writer. She

also came with a wonderful reference from Joan. I thought, 'Great, she can help me to write the colour therapy course; this is what's going to bring in the money to pay for the centre.' I also felt that I didn't know enough, I didn't have enough confidence to do it on my own. But the main problem was that I hadn't learnt to create clear boundaries for myself or for other people: and there are always people who act like parasites on a host. They see they can cross ill-defined boundaries and that's their way in. Then the drama begins. When you find a job done shoddily, you want it done again, but in reality, 'If you wanted a plumber, you should have hired one!' Guilt is also a factor because in a sense you know you're being a cheap-skate, and you let them stay on.

It wasn't all bad news, however. A friend of Ramon's, called Vic, offered to help me with the business side of the centre. At this point he was studying religion at Edinburgh University and seemed very suitable. He also had business experience. Perfect! Now was the time to develop the colour therapy course and I asked Vic to help me. He was one of the most significant people in my life in this respect because in the end he said to me, 'You're not prepared to do it yourself, and I'm tired of waiting for you.' So when he walked out, I felt angry and rejected, and it took the anger in me to make me turn round and say 'Right then, I'll do it.' It was his leaving that provoked me into writing the course myself. It was a major turning point: I finally began to own my vision.

I still needed money, so I rented out Strawberry Bank Cottage again to a woman who came from Inverness. She was able to channel and she channelled Vicky Wall. I found her uplifting and was inspired to see I wasn't the only one doing this sort of work. Her connection to Vicky made her seem immediately acceptable. I imagined she was going to help me run courses and write the literature. Perfect! Again I only saw what I wanted to see and in time, difficulties arose between us because we hadn't laid down clear boundaries.

On another occasion, a young man called Brian arrived wanting a room to rent and I thought he was a really nice guy. Although I knew that he too had a problem with drink and drugs, I also knew he was doing his best to come off them and, as usual, I turned a blind eye. It was the 'woe' in me recognising the 'woe' in him. It's feeling sorry for the underdog, knowing what it's like, which means you don't develop your own self-respect and self-worth. It also makes you feel good, helping people who are down. It's an ego boost, but it's a destructive ego. And so another fish slipped through my net. My turning a blind eye to his problems didn't help him; indeed, my inaction was condoning his behaviour.

The people who came to the centre were often on the dole, or travelling from here to there, wandering around with no money and no job. They were ungrounded, free-flowing, and in many cases, drug users. Like me, they weren't seeing the whole picture. In order for me to see the whole picture, I had to break my life down into segments and look at each individual bit. The people who came to the centre were part of my learning: as long as they appeared to have something to offer, be it help with the plumbing, building, writing or whatever, I let them stay. Part of me was also wanting to be of help, wanting to be liked. The exchange basis for the energy was wrong and in time it turned against me.

During the first few years of people coming to help me there was more a feeling in me of 'Thank God, you've come!' than of 'Thank you God for sending someone'. I believed blindly that everyone who came along had been sent by God to help me. What I didn't realise was that there could be many reasons for people coming here, that God could send people or events for my learning process. Gradually, I began to realise that we can't just blindly wander the labyrinth – God places people on our path for a reason, but it might not be the reason we think it is. I had to learn to take responsibility for my own life and vision. It's fine to have faith in God, which I do, very much, but it's not our faith in Him that makes everything work out the way we want it to. Difficulties and trials come for our own good, to help us evolve. So everyone who came to Firth Lodge had a positive influence. They all taught me something.

I now understand not only the need for clear boundaries but clear communication as well. I thought I had changed from impulsively jumping into things by slowing down my decision-making. I thought that was the issue. I was still looking at how

I could get the best out of these people for the least amount of money. Not out of badness, but because I just didn't have the money.

Vic was the one who got me to understand he would not do it for me. I needed to do it myself. I wrote the course on colour therapy and students began to enrol. I was in business. I had to take on many roles – business woman, mother, teacher, cook, cleaner, writer. Some of these things came more easily than others. For example, I was already a good business woman, dating back to my enterprise selling Mickey Mouse drawings when I was a child. I began to realise I was able to do all these things myself. Much of the time it was trial and error, but at least now I wasn't expecting anyone else to do it for me.

Vicky Wall said to me, 'Never undersell yourself', and I see now that I had been doing exactly that. I didn't have the inner confidence to strike out on my own. It has taken time and many different teachers to bring me to this new level of awareness. Once I had clearly defined boundaries in place, I found that people who in the past had taken advantage of their absence automatically chose to move on. I didn't have to ask them to go on an outer level, because I had done it on an inner level.

A lady called Marilyn Graham came to Firth Lodge as a case history for my electro-crystal therapy thesis. During treatment I had a vision of Marilyn working at the centre. When I told her this she related a similar dream that she'd had. Marilyn came with very clear boundaries and because of this we maintain a wonderful working relationship and friendship.

The journey has been just as important as the vision; and with it, the learning, the evolvement of my being and that of others.

Chapter Thirty-Nine

The day Joan arrived on my doorstep, little did I know the future chain of events that would give me valuable insights into the world of Tibetan medicine and religion.

Joan told me about a Buddhist community called Samye Ling some 80 miles from Auchendinny, in the Borders, and we arranged a visit. It was an impressive place. The first things that caught my eye were the beautiful coloured flags waving in the breeze, and I could hear the gentle tinkling of the wind chimes. The temple was a wonder to behold. Colourfully painted in reds and gold, I had never seen anything like it in my life.

On my third visit to Samye Ling I had a meeting with Dr Akong Tulku Rinpoche, the co-founder of Samye Ling. When we went in to the temple I was told to remove my shoes and I thought, 'Take my shoes off!' I'd gone there with a rather cocky attitude, determined that I was not going to be taken in by any guru figure. Who does he think he is? But when I went into the room I felt an amazing energy. The silence was incredible. I could only feel humbled by the presence of the man. Within the silence I could hear noises and yet they were not of this earth; they were different energies and frequencies. His aura was immense. He sat serenely in a large, comfortable chair. I suddenly found myself sitting completely erect and focused, waiting, hearing my own breathing, almost afraid to breathe. The energy in the room was so great, I felt I could levitate.

Joan broke the silence and spoke. I sat motionless, spellbound in his presence and suddenly he focused on me. He addressed me and asked, 'Why have you come?' From somewhere deep inside I heard my voice, speaking very slowly, calmly and coherently, talking about my vision and the problems I was experiencing. It was almost as if it wasn't my voice – it had a real depth to it. He listened, motionless, and in silence. I finished, confident I had said all I needed to. He smiled and said, 'I shall be the overseer to your project.' And that was it, session finished.

Later, when we met up with Yangdak, a Scottish Buddhist monk who had by now become a friend, he asked, 'How did you get on, Alison, how did you get on?'

I told him, 'Akong Tulku said something about being an overseer to my project, but I don't really know what that means.' Yangdak looked amazed. I said, 'Well, maybe he'll change his mind.' At that, Yangdak grabbed his rosary beads and said a few prayers. He then announced, 'No, he won't change his mind! I think you should know more about Samye Ling and what we're about.'

He took me to his room in which there was a small shrine and he gave me his meditative Tara picture in a frame, saying, 'I want you to have this, it's the one I use everyday.' I was taken aback, because I had christened my daughter Tara. But I knew I had to take it – it was a gift and an honour. With that, I left.

Akong Tulku had asked me to put together in writing a plan for the centre. And so what did I do? True to form, I came back and asked someone else to think it out and put it together. I gave away the responsibility to Vic.

Chapter Forty

In the meantime, I felt it was appropriate for Candy to have some puppies. I found a mate for her and in December 1994 she gave birth. I was running around like a mother hen while the children watched. By this time I was aware that Candy's giving birth was significant in my understanding of my own birth. I knew I would have to give the puppies away, which could well trigger my old feelings of being given away myself. However, everything went smoothly. Candy gave birth to seven beautiful puppies and it was a truly amazing thing to witness. Many visitors came to see the pups and we made up a bed for them in our conservatory. We all took turns to watch over mother and pups.

I almost didn't need to place an advert, as word spread quickly and we found good homes for four of them immediately, but we were left with two dogs and a bitch. I had bred Candy intending to keep a bitch, but the children had fallen in love with the two dogs and not the same ones either! Tara called hers Softy and demanded that we keep him, while Daryl called his Sparky. Meanwhile, they were running amok, tearing the place apart, chewing everything in sight.

One night I was lying on the sofa in the lounge with the lights out, looking through the large panoramic window at the stars twinkling in the sky and I prayed for guidance. I asked God to give me an answer as to what I should do. Two boys and a girl. Which one should I keep and how could I find homes for the other two? Suddenly, a very clear voice said to me, 'You've got to keep the girl.' I was wide awake and immediately replied, 'Well, if I'm to keep the girl, what's her name?' The response came at once: 'Aurora'. And I laughed, thinking with my work, I would have thought Aura would be more appropriate!

I knew Aurora was linked to the stars and the next day I got an encyclopaedia and looked up the Aurora Borealis. I found it to be the Northern Lights, the beautiful coloured lights in the night sky which radiate from the North Pole. I loved the name. It intrigued me and I knew it was somehow connected to my coloured bottles. I told the kids. 'We're going to keep the girl, no arguments, and she is to be called Aurora.

The next day two people rang, both asking for a male puppy, and Sparky and Softy found good homes.

Shortly after this, Aurora became lame. She was unable to run and walked with difficulty. I took her to the vet who took X-rays and did various tests, but nothing came to light. For the next few weeks I was at a loss as to what I could do to help her. One night, Aurora was lying at my feet and my friend John had his easel and paints in the lounge. I had been watching him paint and found myself wanting to paint too, the desire getting stronger and stronger, until I could resist no longer. Intrigued, John watched me as I began to paint.

The painting seemed rather erratic, a dab of colour here, a dab of colour there. I even turned the paper round several times. What was I painting? With a final dab of murky yellow in the middle of the picture, it was finished. I looked at it and thought 'What a mess', and slammed the picture down, disappointed with my efforts. Just as I was about to throw it in the fire, John stopped me. He asked, 'Do you know what you have drawn?'

I replied, 'A mess!'

But he said, 'No, you have drawn Aurora in her aura colours. Have a look. To me, that splodge of pink on her back is a gap in her aura. Her problem is not in her legs, it's in her back.'

I looked at the painting and now saw what John was describing: here was a perfect picture of Aurora, curled up in a ball, sleeping. I was very excited. How could I have done this? But more importantly, I now had the key to what was wrong with her.

The next morning I drove her to John MacManaway, a healer in Fife, who uses massage and manipulation to treat people with back problems, and who also works with animals. I didn't tell him anything about the aura drawing, just that Aurora was lame. He dowsed over Aurora and within minutes, he found a trapped nerve at the exact location of the pink dab in my drawing. He released the trapped nerve using manipulation, and she was better straight away. There has never been a recurrence of the problem.

The next day, the doorbell rang and the girl who rented the stables down the track stood at my door. Hands on hips, she said, 'I believe you dabble.'

'Dabble?' I replied. 'I'm not sure I know what you mean.'

She told me that her horse, Clive, was ill and was going to be put down and could I help. I said I'd try, and followed her down to the stables with my electro-crystal machine. I had been told on my training course that horses could be scanned; however, when faced with this enormous animal, I didn't know where to start. I was frightened. I had no experience of working with horses. As I stood there wondering what on earth I could do, I was suddenly inspired to draw. Tara ran back to the house and brought me her crayons. I asked for guidance and began to draw.

I drew the aura of the horse just like the one I had done of Aurora and, once I'd finished, the colours showed me what was wrong. I could see that energy was being lost from the horse's knees, shown in my drawing as red flashes which also indicated an inflammatory condition. The area relating to the gut was black, and after dowsing for further information I found worms to be the cause. I had coloured Clive's chest area black and his owner confirmed that he'd recently had a chest infection. I drew a black line running from the base of his mane to his tail which was also surrounded by red. I dowsed for more information and found out that Clive had hurt himself six years earlier when he had been in a horse box that overturned. His owner confirmed this, too.

The amount of information gleaned in this aura drawing took me by surprise, while at the same time I tried to act as if it was a normal occurrence. Excited, I telephoned Dr Muriel Mackay and said, 'Guess what I've got this time? A horse! How do I go about detoxing a horse?' Muriel knew, of course, and so we put together a natural healing programme for Clive.

Because of the law relating to the treatment of animals, the first thing I did was buy Clive for a penny, so that legally I could begin treatment. The law states that only vets or the animal's owner can treat an animal. The next thing I did was check what treatment the vet had offered, what the diagnosis and prognosis were. Clive had been given six months to live due to the severe form of arthritis in his knees which meant he would soon be unable to walk and would need to be put down.

I used coloured massage oil, dietary changes, a detoxi-fication programme, electro-crystal therapy, herbs and spiritual healing. Clive loved his treatment and within ten days he was trotting comfortably. Within a month he was rideable and is still alive today, four years on.

Clive showed me that it was possible to decode the electro-magnetic frequency of the aura into a language I could understand. By letting my mind tune into this frequency I had drawn it as different colours which I could translate as illness. By dowsing I could confirm what I had drawn by asking specific questions. All I could think was, 'Thank God, I can now use this "sight" to help me trace the root cause of disease.' And so began the aura drawings and my work with animals.

Tara was with me when I drew Clive's aura and has been present at many of my teachings on the language of colour. She does most of the aura drawings now – usually people send us photographs of their animals and Tara takes her drawings from them.

Chapter Forty-One

For over a year I had been thinking of writing a course in colour therapeutics. I was ready to combine all my knowledge and develop my own way of healing, still focusing on colour therapy, but doing it in a new way. People were already asking me to do workshops and afterwards, when they asked if I ran courses, I had to say no.

One day a medium came to Firth Lodge. She saw the coloured bottles that I was using for my readings and asked me what was wrong with them. I didn't think there was anything wrong with them. But she insisted there was and eventually said to me, 'I have come here to tell you to make your own colour system and your own coloured bottles.' I was amazed. She said, 'Vicky has asked me to give you this message.' Then I recalled what Vicky had said to me the last time we met: 'You will make your own system. Don't ever undersell yourself.' This triggered my recollection of Vicky's visits after her death. For three nights in a row I woke up at about 3 o'clock and there she stood. She told me clearly about certain plants and their colours, and where to find them for healing. She also told me that when I made my own system I should include a bottle with maroon at the top and pink at the bottom and call it the marriage bottle. This has proved to be an invaluable combination for my collection. I knew this woman was right and yet how was I going to do it? It seemed an enormous challenge, bigger than I had ever dreamed of.

Joan then reminded me of the research scientist, Alastair Wilkinson, who had written to me with a sample of a massage oil and said, 'Phone him! He's your man. He will do it.' After some persuasion, I called him, and he was fascinated by the idea. We met to discuss the project and I told him about the coloured bottles and their uses. He agreed to create the bottles of colour – and a new journey began.

This was a difficult journey. It began with 'Where do I start? What do I do? What am I trying to achieve?' Over the next three years I worked on developing the system and gradually it evolved. I knew there had to be a specific number of bottles, but I didn't have a clear idea of how many. I spent much of my time meditating, asking for clarity with this project. There were so many questions to be answered, so much writing: the whole colour system and the definition of each bottle had to be written up; I had to decide which colours and shades to use; which colours to have on their own and which ones to combine, to make the dual-coloured bottles. Slowly it reached completion.

In the summer of 1996, the people who rented Strawberry Bank Cottage decided to clear the steps that lead down to the valley, a job which took them quite a few weeks. Around the same time I was focusing on the number of bottles in the system and the colour combinations, when the number suddenly came to me: 49. There were to be 49 in a set. I called Alastair. 'I have it! It's 49! No more changes. Forty-nine bottles and these are the colours.' Later that day, one of the girls came running up the steps which they had finally cleared. She ran into the house and in great excitement said, 'Guess how many steps there are?' I looked at her enquiringly: '49!', she said. I had been here for four years and it took four years to find out there were 49 steps.

Now that I had finalised the number of bottles and the colour combinations, Alastair started to make them up. I remembered the pyramid Vicky had given me, inscribed with the words 'Success Through Change', and I knew they had to be in pyramid-shaped bottles. I ordered the bottles and produced the first set, which had an amazing impact on me and on many others.

They were my babies and I nurtured them and they nurtured me. They became very special. We took them to exhibitions and used them to do colour readings. People held the bottles and the excitement lighting up their faces reminded me of children having their first ice-cream. At exhibitions our stands were packed and the readings were booked out very quickly. So, as the system evolved, life went on with exhibitions and readings.

Two years earlier a very good friend, who was also a medium, predicted that I would create a system called The Colour Profile Analysis System. I still had to find a name for the bottles, though. I recalled the night I lay in bed and asked God about the puppies. He had said I was to keep the girl and call her Aurora – a name which was connected to the bottles. I had it. The name for the set of 49 pyramid-shaped bottles was to be 'The Aurora Borealis Collection'.

I spent the summer of 1996 writing the brochure about the Aurora Borealis Collection, what it was and how it worked. It amazed me how much work had to be done. I wrote about the property, the Academy of Colour Therapeutics, myself, the children, the people who had helped me. As I did so I glowed with an inner sense of well-being. I was writing, I was being creative. It brought me forward. It raised my self-esteem and self-awareness. By now I had developed a system and named it; developed my own coloured oils; designed the bottles and designed a course to teach students my own system of colour therapeutics. The time for the brochure had well and truly arrived.

I didn't give in to my Gemini nature wanting to have it printed immediately – this time I held back. For two years I held back, both in terms of writing and printing. One of the ideas was to have 'The Scottish Academy Of Colour Therapeutics' on the front of the brochure, but just before it went to print, I realised that the Academy and Good Health For All were really two separate things: the natural healing and spiritual development centre was 'Good Health For All' and had now incorporated 'The Scottish Academy of Colour Therapeutics' within that. From there we began to hold Open Days, Donation Days and Therapist Exchange Days to publicise the variety of holistic treatments we had to offer.

When I first started creating my vision, I didn't think setting up a natural healing and spiritual development centre was compatible with running a business, so I largely ignored the financial side of things relying blindly on God to sort things out for me. I began to realise that 'Good Health For All' and the Scottish Academy of Colour Therapeutics had to be run as a business or they wouldn't survive. Prior to that, I had done many readings for free or as an exchange, but it hardly helped to pay the electricity bill or the mortgage. There had to be a balance.

Chapter Forty-Two

During the time Vic had been at Firth Lodge, he lived in Strawberry Bank Cottage and worked with me as a manager. He put together many different talks and workshops and we travelled through Scotland, visiting a variety of different centres, people and places.

We both worked on the plans for the centre to present to Akong Tulku at Samye Ling. After each new plan was drawn up, which took a lot of work and a lot of discussion, Akong Tulku would say, 'No. You do not have it all yet. Go away and do some more work on it.' With each new plan I believed 'this is it, this plan is now right for him and he will see that', but every time I was told to go away. I wondered what more we could do.

My next thought was that maybe Akong Tulku would buy Firth Lodge. That would be a relief, I thought, get some money in the bank. Again it was my avoidance of owning my vision.

One day my Uncle Charles came to visit and I was telling him about Samye Ling and Akong Tulku. He said very matter-of-factly, 'Oh, I've met him. He was the interpreter for the Karmapa. His holiness, the Karmapa, is the head seat of the Kagupa School of Tibetan Buddhism and is as powerful and respected as the Dalai Lama, except that the Dalai Lama is the overall leader of Tibet and is head of a different school of Tibetan Buddhism.' My uncle was talking about the Karmapa who has since died. Amazed, I listened to his story.

The Karmapa had arrived in Scotland with toothache and was advised through the Embassy to go to my uncle. Having been treated and feeling very pleased to be out of pain, the Karmapa gave my uncle the booklet of his tour. He said that he would bring this brochure to show me and that I could keep it. At that point I wasn't aware of the fact that the Karmapa himself had signed the brochure, so it didn't mean all that much to me.

However, when I went down to Samye Ling for another appointment with Akong Tulku to give him yet another plan, I showed him the brochure with the Karmapa's signature and for the first time, I saw a reaction. He jumped up and said, 'Do you know that this is his actual signature? He has also written a message of thanks.' He was very excited. Usually the Karmapa would travel with a seal which he used instead of signing his name, but this time he had signed his name himself. There are very few documents left with his signature on them as the Chinese had them destroyed. Akong Tulku thanked me for showing it to him and as I left I realised he still hadn't accepted my plan. However, I now knew I had something very special in my possession.

Some weeks later, a friend of mine from Samye Ling, a Buddhist nun, arrived to stay for the weekend. She asked if I had seen Akong Tulku recently with the new plan. I said I hadn't. Since Vic left, I hadn't made up a new plan. She told me that Akong Tulku was leaving Samye Ling on Monday and that I had to see him before he went. I laughed. 'Without an appointment?'

'Yes,' she said.

I drove her back to Samye Ling and on our arrival she ushered me in through the back door, as the front door was locked. I could hear Akong Tulku's voice way down at the end of the corridor and, as I sat waiting with no appointment, thinking he didn't even know I was here, I suddenly remembered I didn't even have a new plan with me. I had nothing. No writing, no thoughts. What would I say to this man? What was I doing here? What was the point? He had so far refused everything I gave him. Then I saw him appear and head for the front door. As he walked past me, I knew the front door was locked and as he turned, I stood up, looked directly at him. I said, 'I am here to see you.'

He said, 'No. I have a meeting now.'

But I insisted, saying 'I have to see you now.' He looked at me and ushered me into his room, and I sat down, praying. I had no idea what I was meant to say.

I found the words, 'I am here. I have no writing, no computer print-outs. I have nothing except me.' At last I was speaking from my soul, not from my head. I carried on speaking, 'I was given a vision of creating a natural healing and spiritual development centre. I don't believe that we can just have the healing without the spiritual development. We need both. We need teachings.' To my surprise, he stood up and shook my hand. He said, 'I grant you a Dharma centre.' He bowed and I bowed. I walked away and wondered, what was a Dharma centre?

As I left I met several people on the way, one of whom said, 'He shook your hand? Let me shake your hand!' My energy soared and I knew the healing centre and the Dharma centre were all one. I had achieved something very great. A Dharma centre is a spiritual teaching centre. I had opened the door and at long last, after two years of plans, I had achieved something that I had almost let go of, thinking it impossible to achieve. Suddenly a yellow ray burst in, the sun shone and my heart soared. I had done it! I thanked God.

I now saw what had been wrong with my plans all along. They hadn't come from my heart, they'd come from my head. Not only that, but they weren't my plans – they were mine and Vic's. I had given *him* my vision to plan and therefore wasn't doing it myself. Vic's leaving led to a period of real growth, for both of us. He had to go his way, and I mine. Our coming together was fruitful in its exchanges of information but I learned the lesson that I had to do it myself. The plan for the natural healing and spiritual development centre had to be composed of my insights, my writings and my work – for a long time I had hoped that somebody else would do it for me, not believing I could do it myself.

Often, being left on your own is an opportunity to develop your own potential. If you are setting yourself up in anything, it is fundamental that your *own* beliefs, writings and teaching come to the fore. My vision could now progress because instead of finding others to do it for me, I was prepared to do it myself.

I set about understanding the wider significance of being a

Dharma centre. I believe that by granting me a Dharma centre, and by giving me his spiritual blessing, Akong Tulku was reinforcing my connection to the universal healing energy. He had seen my dedication and I respect the sacred aspect of what his blessing means. This led me to study my own belief system, which is non-denominational and which forms the basis of my natural healing and spiritual development centre. It is a non-denominational centre dedicated to natural healing and spiritual development.

In 1998 Ramon paid for the old stable to be renovated which saw the completion of the building work on the centre and I am now able to live out the vision fully. I see now that over the seven years since buying Firth Lodge, I have been on a journey of spiritual growth and understanding which has enabled me to clearly see the vision. This in turn has allowed me to bring together both parts, the natural healing and the spiritual teachings.

I now realise the significance of the cycle of seven. I have been working to manifest my vision for seven years. The most vulnerable time was in the middle of that cycle when I could either have given up and lost everything, or kept going. At the end of this seven-year cycle the natural healing and spiritual development centre is ready for its next phase. At 43, my own age cycle is starting again, in harmony with Good Health for All. This is a new beginning.

Chapter Forty-Three

Of all the people who have helped me achieve greater self-knowledge, one of the greatest of these has been my mother, Brenda.

I believe that Brenda was one of the catalysts for my soul's awakening in this lifetime. My soul's awakening allowed me to empty the wastepaper basket, dig deep down and release the anger and frustration – and move on. Brenda came into my life at a very difficult juncture which resulted in my attitude to her blowing hot and cold. I think it was *because* of my conflicting attitude, too, that I didn't want to set up boundaries: I liked to keep situations fluid enough so I could move in and out of them at will. Brenda, faced with my unpredictable nature, tried to overcome it with strict controls, whilst I became angrier and angrier.

For so many years I only saw myself and my anger, I didn't see Brenda. I didn't stop to consider that she had her own history, her own set of worries. I didn't care. It's only in recent years that I've started to ask my mother about her life, her childhood, what she was like as a child, what her lifestyle was like, because I didn't know much about her at all. I never asked.

The focus of our anger is often on the individual who's closest to us, the one who cares most about us. For me, it was Brenda. From the very beginning, I projected all my anger onto her. I didn't see in her the kindness and caring that I see now. She had to take all the blame for my adoption, for Maude's death, for taking my dad away, which couldn't have been easy for her. There was a lot to get through before a proper relationship even started. On reflection, I never saw her as a person, I only saw her as an object on which to vent my anger and she, in turn, was a catalyst to my anger.

One of my greatest awakenings is to the fact that I wasn't quite as innocent as I would have liked to make out. It really did take the two of us to make the relationship so difficult. I gave as good as I got, and yet I looked to her to resolve it: I created a lot of the drama and then shifted the responsibility, as I did for much of my adult life. 'This is your responsibility, you're the adult, you deal with it.' Now I am beginning to take on responsibilities for myself, which means opening up channels of communication and having clarity of thought. I try to see the whole picture and ask 'What are my boundaries, what am I accepting, what am I not accepting?'

I have been very lucky to resolve these issues with my mother while we are both still alive. The question is, what would have happened if she had died before we could resolve our relationship? We often miss the opportunity to resolve things with others because we get stuck in anger, pride, jealousy, hurt and pain. By hanging onto the past, we can't move forward into a healing space. Nevertheless, if someone passes away, leaving unresolved issues, I do believe these can still be healed. It's important to do our own inner work and resolve issues inside ourselves. This can be put out into the universe, transmitted in thought: communication can still be achieved with those who have passed on. If we heal ourselves, that energy will go out to the different planes of existence.

The final communication between my dad and me came after his death, via a medium. And although I didn't know it at the time, his 'sorry' was important. It has allowed me to see our relationship with clarity, to see the imperfections and therefore forgive, and to know that there are no loose ends.

With regard to Maude, I couldn't put her death to rest until I was helped to face it. Once I did that, it opened up new levels of awareness and I began to heal.

With regard to my blood mother, Anne, the 'business' between us ended when I let go of the fantasy image of her. Anne was my birth mother and when I discovered I had been adopted I used her as a weapon against Brenda because I hated Brenda for marrying my father. I had found a way out, a gate:

'I knew you weren't my mother, I've got another mother, a real mother.' I didn't *have* to like Brenda because she wasn't my mother. Anne came into my life with that energy, the energy of my fantasy image of the perfect mother. Suddenly in my mind, I imagined that out there in the world was a woman who was forced to give me up. I worked that fantasy for years until at the age of 24 I first met Anne. For the first six months it was wonderful, until I was faced with the reality of her not being quite so wonderful. I knew there were lies, and that led me to my encounter with Bill, my real father.

Anne and I finished when the illusion was finished. And who did I run to? Brenda.

It was only when I saw through the fantasy picture of Anne that I had created for myself that I was at last able to turn to Brenda as a real mother. I thought, 'Yes, this woman has cared for me, she has tried to teach me her values. Even if, at the end of the day, they aren't the same as mine, she cared enough to want to teach me values.' The most wonderful thing that came out of all that was my realisation that I loved Brenda as a mother and it didn't matter that she wasn't my own flesh and blood. She had shared nearly all of my life, and still does.

Chapter Forty-Four

Over the years I have studied myself and the process of understanding, while at the same time I have become aware of other people's natures. People think in different ways and are at different stages of their evolution.

It began for me with a heart rate peaking at 150 and a sense of total nothingness – and the question of whether I was going to live or die. Somewhere in the depths of my being I realised I had a choice. That choice was to be the basis for my future. It brought with it the will to live and the will to change. I knew part of that process would have to include giving up the things in my life that were destructive, the patterns and conditions, the life style – whether it was wining and dining every night or simply going off on sprees to buy new clothes, toys, objects, furniture or houses.

I have been fortunate in coming into the world with a deep inner faith which I equate to God. I have come to understand that God is within us all: He is our companion, our friend and our teacher. At the lowest ebb in my life I was guided towards aromatherapy, which in turn led me to colour, which finally began the process of transformation. My intuition, my inner knowing and my faith grew. I looked at the patterns of my life and all the things I would have to change and in the process I almost became bankrupt, almost lost my home, and almost lost my life through cancer. I began to stir out of my sleep and see life with more clarity.

I moved to the country with an unshakable belief in a vision to create a natural healing and spiritual development centre. Many times I nearly gave up but, living in a run-down building with no cooking facilities, shower or toilet, I began to see the amazing sunrises and sunsets and the beauty of nature.

Letting go so that change can take place is very difficult. For me, one of the most difficult things has been to let go of the need for others to be in control, be they bank managers, lawyers or possessive husbands. I have had to build my self-esteem and only then, when I took responsibility for myself, did the vision become manifest. It has taken time for me to develop communication with my spiritual helpers but once I allowed them to speak to me, my life became so much easier. I wish I'd listened and trusted them earlier.

Chapter Forty-Five

Ever since I was a little girl I have been able to 'see' things before they happen. I could see colours around people and know if they were going to become ill. What has become apparent to me is that if we have the ability to predict the future, many questions are raised. My thoughts on the matter are that there is a blueprint of future events in the universe. I believe we each have a blueprint of our lives, a map of our destiny.

Because it is a blueprint, I believe we can change that plan to a degree and alter our destiny. We have the free will to make choices, we can go against our destiny or flow with it. We come into this life with an inner knowledge and as children our expressions tend to be free-flowing, but we get channelled in various directions by our parents and society, so that often we lose our pathway. Many people who have issues to deal with as an adult, often find that they stem from their childhood patterns and conditions. For example, a man may be influenced into becoming a doctor because his father is one, but in his true essence, he is an artist. He will then always feel at a loss, unfulfilled, insecure, because he is not fulfilling his own soul's journey. His soul may suddenly wake up and seek to follow its true path or he may have a breakdown, and be forced to change direction. In general, living a false life is too much to take and eventually there will be a breakdown. Outside influences can make or break our lives. We need to be in touch with our own inner, guiding voice.

I think there are many different forces at play, shaping our destiny, and that we are all here to learn. We may make the choice on a personal level to come in and learn something that will evolve us further. So although we choose our pathway, it has many sub-divisions: the external forces of life can affect and alter the details of the soul's journey, but not the journey itself. I think if we were meant to know the full extent of our soul's journey we'd come in knowing it. And if we were meant to remember our past lives we would remember them.

Pathways may be mapped out, and the future already there, but we have free will and within that is our learning process. Stumbling blocks can be turned into stepping stones; learning from a situation can move us on to the next step. It's only when something happens, like when we narrowly escape death, or we meet someone by 'chance' who turns out to have a great influence on our lives, that we think, 'Perhaps there is some greater force at work.' But the forces of destiny are with us every minute of the day – it's just that we're not aware of it until something happens which brings it to light.

There are people who can tell us our destiny, like the medium in Balloch who told Ramon his future and the gypsy who foretold this book. They can see into the future, they're seers. These seers can tap into the universal source of knowledge. When I 'see', everything in front of my eyes goes grey and misty and disappears. I feel as if I am in a time warp, in another dimension. Then I begin to see what could be described as a video tape of future events. What I'm doing is picking up frequencies that are in the atmosphere. In the right frame of mind, in a spiritual frame of mind, it can be tuned into. We can hear things too. We are like a wireless set, picking up frequencies.

Many people become initiated into the spiritual path by their misfortunes. My life prior to my breakdown was spent avoiding responsibility, avoiding anything emotional – it went across the board. It coloured the way I saw men, the way I coped with my children, the way I related to my mother, to everyone. I had no responsibility, I didn't want any. I was always right. I was very angry. I had temper tantrums, I yelled and screamed and shouted. I smoked, I drank, I took drugs, because from a very early age I didn't understand what life was about. I had great difficulty assimilating the structure of having to hoover, having to iron my dad's shirts. When I was a child growing up and was told that this was what I'd be doing as an adult, I thought, 'How depressing, how mundane', but what else was there? You had to go to school and learn, how boring. You had to go and work, how boring. And then you were told you were doing it all because you would soon be 65 and on retirement, receive a pension. And then death. There had to be more than that! But in my day there were no spiritual teachings that I knew about outside the dogma of religion to help me.

I believe that God exists. He's a force that lights our way. This has been true for me. It's our denial of His power that creates difficulties. If we could accept God – and you can put any name to it, call it Universal Energy, whatever – but if more people could accept there's a universal force that we can tap into, great things could be achieved. I believe there is a universal energy flow, there is a rhythm to life, and to the universe. The earth has its own rhythms and cycles and we are part of that.

I am convinced that souls come together and prior to conception there's a soul waiting. I think they choose their incarnation and its duration.

I do think there is a lot more to death and reincarnation than we understand. Genuine mediums who can see into the future, who can give predictions, like Ramon meeting me, our children, the book, the natural healing and spiritual development centre; they're seeing something that is very definitely already mapped out.

To get in touch with the universal force there has to be stillness, quietness, there has to be time for meditation and time for reflection. By sitting still and meditating, sitting quietly and clearing the mind, breathing deeply to relax the brain and the body, we can then get in touch with the Universal Wisdom, or God, within. I think there's a great need for awareness, to keep an open mind. There's no point in saying, 'I can't do anything to help the world', that's nonsense! If everybody said, 'I will donate, I will do, I will join whatever it is to bring about harmony and balance in the world, I will protest against the atrocities, I will challenge' – if everyone does one thing to help, the world would change. A friend of mine fell about laughing once when I was smoking 20-40 cigarettes a day and donated a pound to Cancer Relief. I thought that was all I needed to do, and I plopped a pound in the little box! She said, 'You're the cause of hospitals being overloaded with smoking-related illnesses.' So there is this element in all of us of 'We don't want to do it.' Now that I realise I can make a difference, I do the best I can.

Life is a mystery. There is a way to something higher, deeper, greater and benevolent. Within us all lie the universal secrets, within us all there is God. Within us all is the faint inkling that we have an essential role to play in the world. Each one of us has a road to travel and each one of us can make a difference.

There's an old Chinese saying: 'The wise traveller leaves everything behind; it makes the journey light.'